Albert Schweitzer's Legacy
for Education

Albert Schweitzer's Legacy for Education

Reverence for Life

A. G. Rud

First published in 2011 by
PALGRAVE MACMILLAN®
in the United States – a division of St. Martin's Press LLC,
175 Fifth Avenue, New York, NY 10010.

Where this book is distributed in the UK, Europe and the rest of the world,
this is by Palgrave Macmillan, a division of Macmillan Publishers Limited,
registered in England, company number 785998, of Houndmills, Basingstoke,
Hampshire RG21 6XS.

Palgrave Macmillan is the global academic imprint of the above companies
and has companies and representatives throughout the world.

Palgrave® and Macmillan® are registered trademarks in the United States, the
United Kingdom, Europe and other countries.

ISBN: 978–0–230–10856–1

Library of Congress Cataloging-in-Publication Data

Rud, A. G., 1953–
    Albert Schweitzer's legacy for education: reverence for life/A. G. Rud.
        p. cm.
    ISBN 978–0–230–10856–1 (alk. paper)
    1. Schweitzer, Albert, 1875–1965.   2. Education—Philosophy.   I. Title.
    LB775.S392R83 2010
    370.1—dc22

                                                                    2010023176

A catalogue record of the book is available from the British Library.

Design by MPS Limited, A Macmillan Company

First edition: December 2010

10 9 8 7 6 5 4 3 2 1

Printed in the United States of America.

Permissions

Text in Chapter 9 and elsewhere courtesy Harmony Residential Properties: Restrictions, Guidelines, and Goals Concerning Companion Animals, Habitat, and Wildlife. Harmony Foundation, Inc., and Birchwood Acres Limited Partnership LLLP, ©2002. All rights reserved.

Image 9.1: Schweitzer at Lambaréné, back to camera. Back cover of Finding Lambaréné. Courtesy Marvin W. Meyer. Photograph by Donald Desfor.

Contents

List of Images   ix

Preface   xi

Acknowledgments   xvii

Part I   Schweitzer's Life, Influences, and Convictions   1

1   A Brief Biography of Early Influences   3
2   Schweitzer's Philosophical and Religious Heritage   13
3   An Evolving Relationship: Albert and Hélène   27
4   To Africa: From Thought to Conviction and Action   43
5   Reverence for Life   53

Part II   Schweitzer and Education   65

6   Practical Reverence and Education   67
7   Schweitzer and Moral Education   89
8   Icon, Scoundrel, Prophet, Paradigm? A Recovery
    Project for Schools   107
9   Conclusion: Is the School the Way?   121

Notes   143

Bibliography   163

Index   169

List of Images

3.1   Photograph of Rhena Miller and the author   41

9.1   Schweitzer at Lambaréné   141

Preface

One of the great figures of the last century, Albert Schweitzer, is known chiefly for his humanitarian work as a physician in the African jungle. But his journey there started much earlier, in unlikely circumstances. Schweitzer was a noted Biblical scholar, minister, organist, and author of a number of scholarly works, before he chose to become a medical doctor in early middle age and then go to Africa. Is the work of this man pertinent to a discussion of education in today's world? I argue that Schweitzer's life and work offer both inspiration and timely insights for educational thought and practice in our new century.

Not enough has been done to link and investigate the legacy of Albert Schweitzer for educational theory and practice. For educational theory, I appraise his key theme, Reverence for Life and its educational value, discuss what he meant by making his life his argument, and then inquire about Schweitzer as a prophet for social and educational change. For educational practice, I assess the impact of Schweitzer's thought upon curriculum development, the establishment of schools in his name, and Schweitzer related educational institutes here and abroad.

Schweitzer made a deliberate change in his life's direction in early middle age. He sought personal salvation through his work, deciding to leave his scholarly and artistic life at age 30 to devote himself to service. Schweitzer was deeply concerned about what he saw as a decaying European culture. His contemporary Oswald Spengler's book, *The Decline of the West*, was read widely for its historical dissection of the supposed ills of European culture, as were the more lyrical writings of Friedrich Nietzsche. Schweitzer differed from both these thinkers by making committed action his means of cultural and spiritual regeneration. He stated that he wanted to *make his life his argument*. I use Schweitzer's intellectual heritage to help build my argument for the pertinence of his thought and action for philosophy of education and educational practice.

There has not been a thorough investigation of Schweitzer and education. Ronald L. Abrell wrote three short overlapping articles on this topic.[1]

Abrell saw Schweitzer as deeply concerned about education, but asserted that his educational thought had been overlooked. Schweitzer believed that civilization was in crisis, and could be rescued if the ethic of Reverence for Life was learned by the young.

Schweitzer's decision to go to Africa has perplexed scholars as much as it did his family and close friends at the time. He left his work as a minister, professor, internationally known organist, and Bach scholar to study medicine and go to Africa to found a hospital. This decision seemed sudden to many, especially his family. However, biographical evidence (especially letters recently made public that Schweitzer exchanged with his wife) show that this fateful decision was carefully planned and tied intimately to his view of European civilization and his own religious and philosophical beliefs. Biographical detail here bolsters philosophical analysis of his decision and its relation to education.

Chapter 3 maps the genesis and rationale of his decision to go to Africa through analysis of the letters between Schweitzer and his future wife, Hélène Bresslau, as well as a discussion of interviews I conducted with their only child, Rhena Schweitzer Miller, four years before her death in 2009. I want to know what we may learn about similar, though usually less radical, decisions made by teachers and other educators, as they commit themselves to a life of service. Any such decision has moral importance. Schweitzer turned toward action and to others, seemingly away from the scholarly life per se, though he was able to remain productive as a scholar and artist throughout his life, and gave organ concerts and speeches to raise funds for his hospital.

Analysis of Schweitzer's life and legacy will aid my examination of the formation of character at all levels of education, especially in teacher and leadership preparation programs. Situating his key thought, Reverence for Life, within current educational theory should lead to a beginning and development of Schweitzer educational scholarship.

My initial research has prompted me to think about why Schweitzer's legacy is broad, but not deep, in education. However, I do not intend to contribute simply laudatory efforts to the Schweitzer legend, and I address the Schweitzer of myth and hagiography. There are a number of criticisms of Schweitzer's work that need to be addressed as I construct a more balanced and useful portrait of a man's influence upon education. Schweitzer's educational relevance exists in spite of the passage of time and the cultural differences between his era and our own. The core of his message, epitomized in his declaration that "the school will be the way" is as fresh today as it was in the early part of the last century, particularly for our own educational needs and desires.

I became interested in the life of Albert Schweitzer in the late 1990s. My own research and inquiry into finding ways to learn cooperation and morality from our interaction with animals, particularly pet animals, led me to collaborate with Alan Beck, a friend and noted researcher in Purdue's School of Veterinary Medicine, on the "human-animal bond." I had long suspected that animals were understudied in their relationships to learning, and their ubiquity in children's lives merited further thought. Beck and I focused on the presence of pet animals in schools, and sought to find what was out there in schools in our home state of Indiana, and how animals were actually used in the classroom by teachers.[2] Beck asked if I would be interested in learning more about a start-up project in Florida devoted to establishing a community, with an attached research initiative, on the benefits of animal companionship. I jumped at the opportunity.

The Harmony Institute, whose work in Schweitzer-inspired education I discuss in the final chapter, was unformed and nascent, first just an idea and a small group of people who wanted to foster the relationship between humans and animals, and more widely to enact it as a large community. I had a few years before left another start-up venture, The North Carolina Center for the Advancement of Teaching (NCCAT),[3] where I had been involved in many aspects of institution building. NCCAT is a state-supported and at the time, university-based, institute devoted to the intellectual, professional, and personal renewal of public school educators, particularly classroom teachers but also many other educators, and where we viewed education as occurring in many settings. Teachers, educational leaders, and others discussed wide-ranging topics in a number of fields and engaged in hands-on learning, all within a carefully attended environment. We prized collaboration and creativity, as well as the importance of the calling of the vocation of education, particularly teaching and learning in a supportive environment devoted to growth and knowledge. Another opportunity to be involved from the ground up in an innovative educational venture was irresistible.

The founders of the Harmony Institute, Martha Lentz and her husband, Jim Lentz, envisioned a model way of living in accordance with environmental considerations, as well as keeping a studied, and prominent, place for animals and other living creatures in the community. In addition to a new, planned community of Harmony south of the Orlando (Florida) International Airport and near the towns of Kissimmee and St. Cloud, the Harmony Institute was established to provide research and dissemination on the benefits of the community, with specialists from a wide variety of disciplinary areas devoted to its work. I had helped to develop the philosophy of teaching and learning at NCCAT to encompass a wider sense of where education occurs beyond the classroom. Here at Harmony I saw a similar opportunity, where formal schooling, with its classes and curricula, was embedded in an ecology of learning opportunities in the community. Informing this venture was the example of Albert Schweitzer, especially his famous precept of Reverence for Life.

I knew very little about Schweitzer, at first recalling only a vague image of a kindly looking old man clad in white at work as a doctor in the African jungle. I was only slightly aware of Schweitzer's many accomplishments prior to his work in Africa, and I was unsure how he even had decided to go there. I had sketchy memories of his *Quest for the Historical Jesus* from a freshman course in religion, my eventual college major. Yet I quickly saw the connection between Schweitzer's work in Africa and inspiration for this larger, institutional venture. I became first intrigued, and then beguiled, by his work and example.

As I delved into whatever I could get my hands on about Schweitzer, his work as a theologian and philosopher, medical missionary, and world famous personality, fascinated me on many levels. I had for a long time been interested in how to make one's beliefs and values concrete and especially how to disseminate these ideas in practice. This is a perennial problem for those engaged in educational innovation or reform, as well as anyone pursuing any social change. As a faculty member at NCCAT, I put ideas into practice with satisfying results. I wondered about how much more extensive the work of Schweitzer had been, and was intrigued by what I saw as the finality of his decision to "let your life speak."[4] I was fascinated by what I thought was Schweitzer's distillation of motive and purpose in the larger context of educational purpose and the role of resolve and choice in the lives of educators. I believe there is a continuum of commitment and choice, and I analyze this continuum in later chapters in the context of moral vocation, through a discussion of the moral dimensions of experience.

The sudden and jagged ripping of the social and emotional fabric of my country, brought about by the terrorist attacks of September 11, 2001, and the aftermath of those events, caused me to reflect upon purpose and meaning more sharply. I looked at my own direction in life, and examined my vocation of teaching and writing about educational philosophy. I kept coming back to Schweitzer to help me in this shadowed time. Schweitzer, too, lived through such an age, though even more terror stricken than our own. I sought this voice of someone who had "been there," and who could show me a more productive and satisfying way to look at life.

I saw that Schweitzer's ideas on education were compatible with my own, but that his life and his thought had only been examined inchoately and sometimes briefly as sources of inspiration and practical ideas for education. I soon realized that he was difficult to emulate or follow, but that his educational legacy could be studied more, adapted, and even extended. Schweitzer was able to follow through from what had been a very early commitment to not harm living things, and to live in accordance with the demand of a conscience, a duty toward others fueled by his religious belief and philosophical convictions. Schweitzer counts a number of incidents in his life as important turning points, and he is not doubtful about them. I begin with a discussion of his youth, particularly his most meaningful formative relationship, with his future wife, Hélène Bresslau. I describe these events in the first part and link them to educational theory and practice in the second part of the book.

The book is divided in two parts. In Part I, I reflect upon Schweitzer's life and accomplishments, and describe his influence. In Part II, I delineate his educational legacy in moral education and in what I call practical reverence. I return to a critical examination of Schweitzer's legacy, assessing its limitations and opportunities. Schweitzer's work is a testament of hope, and so I end by discussing what we may take away from this legacy today, especially for teaching and learning both inside and outside schools.

Acknowledgments

This book germinated and bloomed slowly. Fits and starts, delays in writing other things, a sometimes stymied imagination, a daughter to see through college and launch toward her own Lambaréné, and stimulating yet demanding positions in academic leadership are not entirely conducive to sustained manuscript preparation. I could have said "No, thanks. I must finish my book" to many requests and expectations on my time, and alas I did not. I have no regrets.

Through it all there was the loving inspiration, and in the end, expert editing of my wife Rita. I also felt the love and support of our daughter, Rachel, and my parents, the late Anthony G. Rud and Marianne E. Rud. Friends and colleagues likewise lifted me along the way: Alan Beck, Michael Bérubé, George Bodner, Nick Burbules, Jack Fenner, Jim Garrison, Gene Glass, David Granger, Jim Greenan, David Hansen, David Ives, Nathalia Jaramillo, Jiwon Kim, Anne Knupfer, Martha Lentz, Bill McInerney, Marv Meyer, Patti Marxsen, Jo Palmieri, Ryan Schneider, Len Waks, and Cliff You. At Palgrave Macmillan, Burke Gerstenschlager, editor, and Samantha Hasey, editorial assistant, saw value in this project and guided it to completion. Purdue University, its College of Education, and my colleagues in the Department of Educational Studies, as well as the American Studies Program of the College of Liberal Arts, always provided a scholarly and supportive environment. In the final stages of manuscript preparation, my new institution, Washington State University and its College of Education, offered much needed support.

Part of Chapter 6 is adapted from A. G. Rud and Jim Garrison, "Leading Schools with Reverence," *Educational Forum* 74(2) (2010): 143–57; and Jim Garrison and A. G. Rud "Reverence in Classroom Teaching," *Teachers College Record*, 111(11) (2009): 2626–46. Part of Chapter 7 is adapted from A. G. Rud, "Caring for Others as a Path to Teaching and Learning: Albert Schweitzer's Reverence for Life," in *Ethical Visions of Education: Philosophies in Practice*, edited by David T. Hansen (New York: Teachers College Press, 2007), 157–71. Part of Chapter 9 is adapted from A. G. Rud, "Albert Schweitzer's Legacy for Educational Theory and Practice," in

Reverence for Life Revisited, edited by David Ives and David A. Valone (Newcastle, UK: Cambridge Scholars Publishing, 2007), 161–69, and an unpublished response I delivered to papers by Paul Smeyers and David Bridges on "Government Intervention in Areas of Child-Rearing" at the *Educational Theory* Summer Institute, University of Illinois, July 2009.

Part I

Schweitzer's Life, Influences, and Convictions

1

A Brief Biography of Early Influences

A biography can begin to reveal motivation and character, but one must be careful of making too many assumptions based on one's early life. It may be too easy to attribute later action to early incidents or to one's parents, teachers, or siblings. However, early influences can be critical in one's life outlook, and for someone with precocity of habit and manner as Schweitzer, these influences can reveal some clues about his life trajectory. He wrote of his formative early years and how life in Europe shaped his path taken later in Africa where he had made his major life choice. Schweitzer is remarkable in how he sees aspects of his character crystallized in particular incidents of his childhood. These incidents built the foundation of his character for later analysis of his thought and action in Africa as well as his legacy for educational theory and practice.

I give this brief biography of Schweitzer's early life in this chapter for a number of reasons. First, the foundation and development of his life and his educational views are foreshadowed by visiting childhood influences. This portrait comes not only from his words, but also from several noted biographies. Second, discussion of his biography is useful in assessing its sphere of influence upon current educational practice. This idea forms the basis for discussing later in the book Schweitzer as possibly a paradigmatic figure in the sense of that term given by the philosopher Karl Jaspers, as well as an educational prophetic figure in the sense of that term given by the educational philosopher David Purpel.

Schooling and Family

Many of us trace aspects of our character back to our childhood, where our ideas and behavior are being formed by family and influential authority figures in the community, such as teachers, religious leaders, and such. Often, it is not appropriate to draw any sort of definite conclusion from one's childhood on which to base adult motivation and behavior. Freud sought the roots of adult behavior in childhood incidents and practices with a sweeping generalization that is stimulating to read and ponder but is questionable regarding individual cases. That I like an orderly life may not be causally related to my potty training, but may have other roots that we are just beginning to explore in the neurosciences. Much ink has been spilled in linking both traumatic and pleasurable incidents in childhood to patterns of adult behavior. However, if I do *believe* that potty training affected how I conduct my later life, then that is pertinent and illuminating to *how* I see my life. Others may question the interpretation given by the adult, as I will later do with how Schweitzer saw his life and, indeed, how others constructed a life story for him. With Schweitzer, early incidents remain pertinent and relevant, particularly since he has authored his own published narrative, and thus we must, at least at first, take these to be how he interpreted these early life incidents and how they fit into his narrative.[1]

A number of influences and in particular character making incidents from his childhood molded the outlook of Schweitzer later in life. There are certain developments during Schweitzer's childhood that he recounts and that are discussed by several biographers. On his early accomplishments as a scholar and musician, I rely upon his own words of description, as well as those of several biographers. In Chapter 3 his premarital relationship with Hélène Bresslau, revealed in the published letters between them covering their long friendship, courtship, and finally marriage, forms the basis of my investigation.

Early Life

Albert Schweitzer was born in 1875 in Alsace, a region between Germany and France known for its internationalism and its resistance to being either German or French entirely.[2] He was the son of Louis and Adèle Schweitzer. Louis Schweitzer was a pastor and cast an important influence upon his son's upbringing. The key factors in Schweitzer's childhood were the religious tradition in which he was raised, his awareness that he was the son of a pastor, as well as the peaceful countryside of Alsace. They all helped to shape his outlook.

Alsace was the geographical anchor for him even as he spent most of his life elsewhere. It is an area that changed hands four times between Germany and France in the first half of Schweitzer's life, and numerous times during the several hundred years before his birth. Kaysersberg, where Schweitzer was born, and Günsbach, where he grew up, were and are now small villages in the Colmar region of the province. This area was predominantly agricultural when Schweitzer grew up there in the late nineteenth century. While the region is largely Roman Catholic, the Protestant denominations, such as Lutherans and Anabaptists, have played an important role in history. Schweitzer would have been familiar with the Mennonite sects there, and it is here in Alsace that Jacob Amman broke away from the Mennonites, and his followers were later called the Amish.

Later, Schweitzer would have his only child, his daughter Rhena, educated by the Moravian brethren called the Herrenhüter. This simple piety of the Brethren of the Moravian church lived on "with a three-fold ideal of faith, fellowship, and freedom, and a strong emphasis on practical Christian life rather than on doctrinal thought or church tradition."[3] The Moravian bishop Johann Amos Comenius, discussed in Chapter 3, preserved these values in his educational philosophy and practice that included schools imbued with this faith and a belief in dialogue and reason as a means to achieve international peace.

Schweitzer seemed a misfit in a traditional educational setting. While he constantly questioned his elders; he would persist to an unusual degree in the philosophical queries that characterize many young searching souls. Suffering bothered him tremendously, especially that of animals, though he was capable of inflicting pain upon animals, which led him to guilt and further questions. As James Brabazon notes, he looked to philosophy and religion to provide the answers to these questions: "Where does pain come from? Why is it necessary? And what philosophy or religion could explain it and give the world a true ethical basis for dealing with it?"[4] As he entered adolescence, his love of music became central, particularly the playing of the organ. Yet, Schweitzer very much wanted to be like a villager, and in *Memoirs of Childhood and Youth* he writes at some length about the various ways that he did this—what food he ate, the kind of clothing he wore, and so forth—in order to try to fit in with others. He was stung by the fact that even if he did all this, he still was not accepted by the boys in the village. He did not want to be perceived as being the son of a pastor and thus some-how better than others. In other respects, Schweitzer seems to have had an ordinary childhood. He recalls vividly the task of writing thank-you notes for gifts, and how onerous this was, especially since all the children had to assemble in their father's study, and attend to the task until completion. He remembers being fond of the village school, especially Father Iltis, from whom he learned a great deal "without exertion,"[5] a sentiment not extended to all his teachers.

Schweitzer had a strong and humble sense of equality. However, he did differ from his classmates in his marked sensitivity to suffering, whether it was by downtrodden humans or hapless animals. There are a number of well-known incidents that he recounts from his childhood to illustrate that sensitivity. These have become part of the Schweitzer legend that has perpetuated in part by his deeds but also, as here, his recounting of his own moral narrative; it is worth considering them anew as a foundation for our later discussion of his evolving motivation to go to Africa, and what he considered educational aspects of his development.

Schweitzer was saddened and disgusted by the old horse beaten on its way to slaughter.[6] Later, in Africa, he noted the same treatment of animals. Yet he was acutely aware of his own delight as a boy in such activity. While many children, particularly boys, tease animals and are even cruel to them,[7] few remember such incidents as important or key to the development of their personality. Schweitzer focuses on these few incidents to a degree that shows they helped constitute his outlook later for reverence for life. He recalls vividly his delight in disciplining Phylax when the dog chased after the postman.

> What a proud feeling it was to stand in front of the barking, snarling dog like a lion tamer and master him with blows when he wanted to break out of the corner! That proud feeling did not last, however. When we were later sitting together as friends, I reproached myself for having beaten him. I knew I could keep him away from the mailman by holding his collar and stroking him. Nevertheless, when the critical hour approached, I yielded again to the intoxication of playing a tamer of wild beasts.[8]

Schweitzer remembered these incidents and is frank about how he participated in them. He is candid and vulnerable, showing that he too had these all-too-human feelings. Schweitzer thought of himself as a master of a defenseless creature, and it "intoxicated" him. For some people, the experience of having dominion over creatures continues to cloud their perceptions and may lead to other kinds of abusive behavior.[9] For Schweitzer, it led to shame and a resolve to do better.

A key incident

The most vivid incident in Schweitzer's childhood shows not only his sensitivity, but indicates the beginnings of his principle of attention to all forms of life that would later develop into reverence. This final story is stirring, and has been portrayed in the Academy Award–winning documentary on Schweitzer.[10] Let us look carefully at how Schweitzer tells this story to see what it can reveal about his character, particularly his outlook on moral commitment and his resolve, and then briefly compare it to the cinematic treatment. Here is his description of the incident:

> We approached a leafless tree in which birds, apparently unafraid of us, were singing sweetly in the morning air. Crouching like an Indian hunter, my friend put a pebble in his slingshot and took aim. Obeying his look of command, I did the same with terrible pangs of conscience and vowing to myself to miss. At that very moment the church bells began to ring out into the sunshine, mingling their chimes with the song of the birds. It was the warning bell, half an hour before the main bell ringing. For me, it was a voice from Heaven. I put the slingshot aside, shooed the birds away so that they were safe from my friend, and ran home. Ever since then, when the bells of Passiontide ring out into the sunshine and the naked trees, I remember, deeply moved and grateful, how on that day they rang into my heart the commandment "Thou shalt not kill."
>
> From that day on I have dared to free myself from the fear of men, and when my innermost conviction was at stake, I have considered the opinions of others less important than before. I began to overcome my fear of being laughed at by my classmates. The way in which the commandment not to kill and torture worked on me is the great experience of my childhood and youth. Next to it, all others pale.[11]

The portrayal in the film is hushed with the exception of the small boys talking. We see it from an outsider's, omniscient point of view, rather than that of Schweitzer as in the memoir above. We hear the pealing of the bells and see how young Schweitzer upsets the hunt. The camera tightly focuses on his face, and shows the birds fluttering away. The church bells are loud and oracular. That this incident is so portrayed indicates how central the filmmaker regards it to Schweitzer's development of character, and here there is agreement between the film and the memoir.

Why does Schweitzer regard this incident as the most significant of his childhood? He decided on his own to stand up for what he believed about other living things, but we can't say that he necessarily thought this; this is a clue to why this is a central incident. The realization came to him in an emotionally charged moment. It is almost as if he was *called* to this. There is a sense of an involuntary pull toward something else, and for Schweitzer, and for the viewer of the film, this pull is signaled by the pealing of the bells. Something higher, beyond a particular incident and beyond what his friend may have thought which was painful too, came to him even as

Schweitzer wanted desperately to fit in with the neighborhood boys. He has this revelation, and it connects an incident (the slingshot), an image (the bird in the tree), a sound (the bells), and something that associates with that sound (a dictum). This powerful mnemonic carved its place in his heart and his mind. He learned that he had the resolve to stand up against this kind of action.

These experiences, including several dominating horses and delighting in snagging fish, engendered for Schweitzer shame and thoughts that we all experience: "From such experiences, which moved my heart and often put me to shame, there slowly arose in me the unshakable conviction that we may inflict death and suffering on another living being only when there is an inescapable necessity for it and that we must all feel the horror of thoughtlessly killing and causing pain."[12] His reflection is powerful and final, though measured. It is only "inescapable necessity" whereby we can "inflict death and suffering on another living being." This thought would guide him in his medical work in Africa, as well as his opposition to atomic weapons late in life.

Schweitzer also believed that animals exhibited an ethical regard toward each other, and cites observations to support a view that is gaining increasing attention today.[13] Though he is not certain that such behavior is definitive, he believes it points toward a natural regard that especially parents have toward the young. A flock of geese waits for a fellow goose whose wings were clipped by a gardener until its wing feathers had grown enough for flight; monkeys adopt an orphan among their midst; an injured sparrow is allowed to get its fill of crumbs undisturbed by fellow healthy birds.[14] The experiences were both moving and shame producing. Schweitzer believes that such a feeling is universal, but is ignored or swept aside by either aversion to being thought too sentimental, but also, more importantly, he concedes that we "allow our feelings to be blunted."[15] In talking about Dr. Wehmann, a great influence upon him and a man who later committed suicide, Schweitzer says: "Through him I gained an insight which I have tried to apply in my work as an educator: that a profound sense of duty pervading even the slightest detail is a great educational force which accomplishes what no exhortations or punishments can achieve."[16] Schweitzer believed, as did Immanuel Kant—the philosopher he admired greatly—that ethical regard grew and resided within, in the sense of duty engendered by an education, rather than with any consequence, external reward, or punishment.

This indirect way of teaching Schweitzer speaks about is through example. As with the quotation before, it is terse and calls out for explication. Schweitzer admires here an unwavering sense of duty. But, to whom or what is this duty? It seems that here he is praising constancy of character. External guides to character, such as exhortations and punishments, are not as effective as an educative influence. Finally, we see here that Schweitzer does not characterize himself as a physician, but as an educator. How is it that he is educating? It is through the active life (Schweitzer wrote these words 10 years after he first went to Africa) of helping others, and showing by example, that Schweitzer is accomplishing his teaching, much the way that Dr. Wehmann made such an indelible impression upon him.

Coupled with this belief in the importance of the example of duty is Schweitzer's allegiance to reason, even in matters of religion as he was a follower of Kant and the Enlightenment. However, here Schweitzer is holding incompatible thoughts, namely the power of the example of duty, and the need to understand all with reason. He discusses his differences with Pastor Wennagel, who affirmed the supremacy of faith over reasoning: "I, however, was convinced, and still am, that it is precisely through reasoning that the fundamental ideas of Christianity have to be confirmed. Reason, I told myself, has been given to us so that we may grasp through it all thoughts, even the most sublime ones of religion. This certainty filled me with joy."[17] Schweitzer took a path toward a rational faith that would lead him to a synthesis similar to that of Hegel and Spinoza, and would allow him to be open to other traditions—in particular, Jainism—and to support his views on the sanctity of life. This path is remarkable and contrary to the immediacy of faith that he experienced as a Christian. He was a man who affirmed a rational faith, was open to and intellectually curious about other religions, but at his core was a man who wanted to follow simply the example of Jesus, and set out to do just that in his work in Africa.

The sensitivity Schweitzer displayed in the incident with the slingshot and the bird was tempered by the other great formative influence upon his life, music. He began playing the piano and the organ as a young boy, and devoted most of his attention in life to the organ and to his favorite composer, Johann Sebastian Bach. He was to draw deep sustenance from Bach, and impressed his teacher, the great organist Charles-Marie Widor, with his interpretation of the literary and emotional aspects of Bach's music that ran counter to the purely formalistic and mathematical appreciation current in the day.[18] Though he thought he would have to abandon his musical career when he went to Africa, his devotion to the art continued such that he played organ concerts, continued to write about Bach, and even conducted research and wrote articles and books on the preservation of older organs and the changes in the practices of constructing organs. He had a special piano outfitted for the extremely humid climate of Lambaréné that he played late at night after his work in the hospital.

Schweitzer's need for and appreciation of artistic expression was not limited to music or natural beauty. He remembers the effect of Bartholdi's sculpture in Colmar upon him, and how he often visited it. There, a massive statue of a reclining African native exuded strength and solidity of character. Yet for Schweitzer this brooding man seemed to bear the weight of that continent upon his shoulders: "It is a Herculean figure with a thoughtful, sad expression. This Negro gave me a great deal to think about. Whenever we went to Colmar, I sought an opportunity to look at him. His face told me about the misery of the dark continent. To this day, I make a pilgrimage to see him when I am in that town."[19]

Schweitzer comes again and again in these memoirs to the primacy of direct and fresh experience. He liked his studies in the sciences, but not because of the textbook presentations. The kind of awe he felt for Nature was all but dried up in a textbook.

> Their confident explanations formulated for memorization—which, I noticed, were already somewhat outdated—did not satisfy me in any way. It seemed ridiculous to me that wind, snow, hail, rain, the formation of clouds, the spontaneous ignition of hay, the trade winds, the Gulf Stream, thunder and lightning were supposed to have been explained. . . . It wounded me that the ultimate mysteriousness of nature was not recognized and teachers confidently claimed to have an explanation where only a more deeply penetrating description had been achieved; this made the mysterious only more mysterious.[20]

The same kind of teaching robbed Schweitzer of the joy of Homer's epic poems, as the students would have to learn labyrinthine genealogy[21] or trivia such as how Achaean boats were beached.[22] Pedantic teaching took away the life of these books, much as the slingshot could take away life from the bird he and his friend hunted in his youth.

Forming an Outlook

In looking back upon his life, Schweitzer notes the central incidents that helped to form his outlook. He was conflicted in being the son of a pastor, which the local boys saw as being better than them, or so Schweitzer thought. He was sensitive to the suffering of others, especially animals, and as he became older, people; this he imagined was the case with Bartholdi's African. These early influences joined with his study, especially of religious and philosophic traditions. Schweitzer famously proclaimed "Wir epigones," that we are merely fleeting and exhausted remnants of a spent civilization. He saw the way out of these shadows through a commitment to action that occupied most of his life. But Schweitzer did not leave these intellectual and religious traditions behind when he studied to become a medical doctor and then went to West Africa to practice among the native people. He fused these traditions with his work to form his distinct contribution to active and committed thought in practice, with its impact upon many fields, including education.

2

Schweitzer's Philosophical and Religious Heritage

Education consists in this, that the entire domain of human knowledge is comprehended in its basic outlines and that this should form a single world view bringing the individual into conscious relationship with his surroundings and determining his opinions and his activities. Deep in the heart of man lies this yearning for a world view. The sciences as such can never free him; only philosophy has this possibility . . . So it is wholly false to say that philosophy has outlived its day. Without philosophy no education is possible and without education there can be no ethics and no religion in a scientific era.[1]

Schweitzer learned from and responded to a philosophical and religious heritage that formed his thinking as much as his personal associations and childhood formed his character. He was educated to be a philosopher and a theologian, saw the cultural forces at work in his time, and gave a distinctive answer and reaction to the currents of his age. I shall first discuss his philosophical heritage with Kant, Goethe, Schopenhauer, Nietzsche, and Spengler. These thinkers were part of the intellectual climate of Germany at the time and Schweitzer read them and absorbed their influences into his own outlook and thought. However, he went beyond their thinking in important ways in his life and in his intellectual work, by joining this German thought with that of Christianity and Jainism. The intellectual and religious heritage and traditions that Schweitzer brought to bear upon his work and that we can bring to bear upon teaching, learning, and leading in education are rich and deep.

Immanuel Kant

Schweitzer wrote his doctoral dissertation about the work of Immanuel Kant. For the young Schweitzer, the lure of the eighteenth-century thinkers, especially

Kant, was their rationality, which goes beyond tradition and circumstance to the ideal. Kant responded to the great debates of early modern philosophy about the source, scope, and limits of human reason with a new synthesis of reason and experience. James Brabazon comments upon how Schweitzer felt at home in this eighteenth-century synthesis: "He liked the eagerness for truth and justice that he found in the philosophers of that period, and he wanted to know why it had now dwindled into disillusion and skepticism."[2] This theme, of enlightenment dimmed and a spirit exhausted, pervades Schweitzer's work and worldview, and is central to understanding his particular response to overcoming these tendencies in the world he inhabited.

Schweitzer was drawn to Kant's thought regarding the scope and limitations of reason for more than academic or intellectual reasons. He had a deeply personal connection to the philosopher's project. He saw how Kant circumscribed reason's influence thus making it a powerful tool that led, he thought, to a regeneration of culture based upon aiming reason more toward the works of human beings. But what really impressed Schweitzer most about Kant's project was its persistent search, through the process of critique, for the fundamental basis for right conduct. Practical reason for Kant rested upon his categorical imperative, to act only on a basis that you can will to become universal law. Schweitzer wanted also to find a core principle upon which to base his life. The attraction of Kant would be to this aspect of his thought, the moral thinking of his work, *Critique of Practical Reason*. But it was what Schweitzer saw as the moral intuition of duty that made Kant a "Christmas friend," someone he remembered fondly one holiday season as he wrote about his work, in spite of Schweitzer's criticism of the scholasticism of Kant's argument. There, beneath the dry metaphysical discussion, Schweitzer saw a bedrock value of the moral law that was an anchor for Kant's thought.[3] Kant's abstractions were unnecessary to Schweitzer's view of ethics. The categorical imperative of acting so that the maxim of your action becomes a universal law is a standard by which a life can be lived. Schweitzer wanted this kind of standard, and he used it to judge what had been done. Some people are puzzled when they hear that Schweitzer called his life project, the hospital in Lambaréné, an "improvisation." But Schweitzer was being true to Kant's ethics here. All the good works that he did over the 52 years he was there did not make him "moral." The standard and inspiration for morality was present elsewhere, in an inner sense of duty that both Kant and Schweitzer recognized.

Johann Wolfgang von Goethe

As Kant's moral law deeply influenced Schweitzer, so did the wide ranging inquiry and artistic achievements of Johann Wolfgang von Goethe, and it is to Goethe that Schweitzer was continually attracted. He writes to the editor and translator of his studies on Goethe, "Goethe is the personality with which I have been most deeply concerned. . . . What attracts me in him is that he is a man of action at the same time that he is a poet, a thinker, and in certain domains a savant and a man of research. And what binds us together in the deepest depths of our beings is his philosophy of nature."[4] Both men were skeptical of philosophical abstractions. As Brabazon notes, "Nothing was ever purely cerebral for Schweitzer. Other philosophers could, and often did lead lives that appeared to be totally unaffected by their theories and speculations. Not so with Schweitzer."[5] Goethe even expressed that he simply did not understand the speculative philosophy of his day, thought Kant's *Critique of Pure Reason* was a prison, and insists in one of his epigrams that he has never reflected upon thinking.[6] Charles Joy says of Goethe in his introduction to Schweitzer's lectures on him that "[m]an's noblest experience is that of awe, and if the phenomena as such are awe-inspiring, let him be content. He will mount no higher; he should not try to get behind the experience."[7] Goethe was puzzled about discussions of ethics, thinking them dry, pedantic, and removed from life's concerns. He solved the old "is/ought" dilemma of ethics; namely, how can one derive an ethical claim from Nature, simply by declaring his belief in natural revelations of ethics *in* Nature.[8]

Schweitzer returned to think about Goethe at different stages of his life. He saw three main motifs in Goethe's thought and example and these are important to understanding Schweitzer's own intellectual and practical path in life: "the growth of nobility, the refining influence of woman, and the consciousness of guilt."[9] One becomes noble through action, a manner of ethical purification. This path is abetted by the presence of woman, in Goethe's life and in his literature. Indeed, what Schweitzer says about Goethe he thinks equally applies to his own character and outlook: "He consecrates woman as the one who helps to achieve nobility and to guard nobility, because she fulfills this mission in his own life."[10] In the following chapter, we shall see how such thought resulted in commitment to action through a long friendship, courtship, and finally marriage to Hélène Bresslau. Schweitzer relied on the idea of Kantian duty, and coupled that with a demand upon for action in the world. In Goethe's *Wilhelm Meister's Journeyman Years, or the Renunciants*, the protagonist visits the Pedagogical Province and there too has a moment when he is instructed to see a core idea of life, that of reverence. Unlike Schweitzer's idea of Reverence for Life, which comes as a revelation, Wilhelm is coaxed somewhat didactically by another to recognize a threefold reverence, for that which is above, around, and below, and out of it comes the reverence for oneself.[11]

In Kant's moral writings, Schweitzer saw a fellow spirit seeking the grounding intuition for how to live an ethical life. In Goethe, Schweitzer saw reflective action conditioned by reverence. Goethe's idea of threefold reverence in *Wilhelm Meister* is tantalizingly similar to Schweitzer's own idea of Reverence for Life, but Goethe's idea does not consider the natural world, and Schweitzer distinguishes his own idea from it and denies that Goethe is an influence:

> I have always been disturbed by the passage concerning the threefold reverence, because Goethe deals superficially with it instead of going to the bottom of the matter. This passage has always irritated me. The idea of reverence for life came to me as an unexpected discovery, like an illumination coming upon me in the midst of intense thought while I was completely conscious. And when the idea and the words had come to me, it was of Buddha I thought, and not of Goethe.[12]

Schweitzer saw the lessons of *Wilhelm Meister* coming not from artificial presentations of ideas, but in his character development:

> The ethical thinking of Goethe is completely expressed in the fact that Wilhelm Meister, the character which most reveals his personality, is moved, by his inner experiences and by the circumstances of his life, to devote himself to others and to offer his services as a surgeon to emigrants.[13]

Inner moral development, the work of the soul in reflecting upon choice, obligation, and responsibility, coupled with how one approaches what life offers, is the guidance that Schweitzer takes from Goethe, rather than what he considers the superficial idea of reverence in *Wilhelm Meister*.

Freidrich Nietzsche

It was against this backdrop that Schweitzer looked upon the thought of Friedrich Nietzsche, whose idiosyncratic vision of philosophy and religion Schweitzer reacted to at the same time as he shared Nietzsche's criticism of the values of late-nineteenth-century Europe. Nietzsche drew upon the pessimism of Arthur Schopenhauer, and especially his philosophy of the will, to formulate a philosophical position that elevates vitality and artistic expression. Schopenhauer intrigued Schweitzer for his use of Indian thought, but Schweitzer was entirely dissatisfied with what he saw as Schopenhauer's passivity and acceptance of the world, as well as his pessimism. Schweitzer countered the Schopenhauerian pessimism of Nietzsche, but did so with an optimism born of action in the world as a means to overcome spiritual decay. This action is the meaning of making your life your argument. Schweitzer's criticism of Schopenhauer and Nietzsche is twofold and unique. Schweitzer's 50-plus years in Africa, where he constructed a hospital and ministered to the sick for many years, before his own narrative began to be written as either hagiography or as damning criticism by others, is his response to the pessimism of Schopenhauer and by extension Nietzsche, Spengler, and other thinkers who dissected what they saw as a spent civilization. Schweitzer had more to say about Nietzsche.

Nietzsche saw that European thought had gone down a path that led to a desiccated place where reason had cleared the landscape of anything that might approach what he deemed noble human accomplishment, and had led to an era of common sameness and, quite frankly, democracy. Nietzsche ennobled the artist and the insightful intellectual. He delighted in his own written creations and dared others to think like him. He proclaimed the death of God, but privileged human will to power. Nietzsche's thought is complex and contradictory, and I will focus on only three aspects of it in relation to Schweitzer: spiritual decay, individualism, and prophecy.

Spiritual Decay

Nietzsche looked around at the cultures and societies of late-nineteenth-century Europe and saw that as a result of an Enlightenment thinking tradition had corroded and a vibrant life of action and artistic achievement was absent. In his earlier work, he set the opposition in terms of ancient Greek culture, where the "Apollonian" light of reason caused one to dissect, to verbalize, and to not act. The Hegelian owl of Minerva flies at twilight, meaning that reason's reflection occurs only after action and cultural products, and where philosophers parasitically interpret what has already happened rather than give life to a new culture or a new social order. Nietzsche's response to that is on the one hand a virtuoso and lyrical prose that uses narrative in its attempt to reignite culture, and on the other a deep pessimistic individualism that leaves little room for individual action and amelioration of suffering by others. Schweitzer was as interested and passionate as Nietzsche in wanting to make alive a new culture to replace one that was moribund, but the path he took toward that end could not have been more different. Schweitzer turned outward toward others, and more importantly, recognized the pain and suffering in his immediate surroundings, and worked in a practical manner toward its erasure. He took exactly what Nietzsche saw as the weak abdication of

Jesus of Nazareth and his followers as a virtue, seeing instead boundless sacrifice and service.

Individualism

Nietzsche's emphasis upon the individual is evident in the content and style of his writings. He speaks of the "will to power" as the solution to overcome cultural ills, and looks to his own work as proof of his ability to comprehend and recommend change. Schweitzer did not think of his own work as an individual effort, even as he took the initiative to establish the hospital. Though he could be a difficult and imperious task-master, he saw himself as serving others in Africa. However, in his own way, Schweitzer too was enacting Nietzschean individualism. As Mark E. Jonas states, "The strong individual self-if she is truly strong-will not try to abdicate her self-identity as if it were a mask, but will find ways to make her self-identity stronger."[14] I agree with Jonas's interpretation of Nietzschean self-overcoming as self-mastery, and see that Schweitzer really was affirming Nietzsche's idea of self-mastery, and of reason as a type of passion.[15] Schweitzer's self-mastery manifested itself in his concrete and outwardly directed action, through reason and the affirmation of Reverence for Life, a goal which, as Jonas puts it regarding Nietzsche's view of the sublimation of power "is to "say yes" to life, to love and revere life-affirming expressions of power."[16] Schweitzer was seeking ways to serve others in need, not as a pastor or teacher, where he felt suffocated by a life he believed did not have consequence. The opportunity to serve others in a robust and life-affirming manner first presented itself when he discussed the Paris Missionary Society and the needs in equatorial Africa with Hélène.

Prophecy

In Chapter 8 I characterize Schweitzer as an educational prophet, develop-ing that idea from thinkers in educational philosophy who see teaching as a calling or vocation, and the role of the teacher being someone who bears witness to cultural lassitude and social injustice by pointing to a better place and how we educators can get there. Here suffice it to say that both Schweitzer and Nietzsche were prophets, but of a different sort. Nietzsche's reaction to what he saw as a compromised and dying culture was to assert the power of the irrational Dionysian force at the core of life. He used the legendary character Zarathustra to talk about what had been lost in European culture through the procession of Enlightenment reason and the history of Christianity, and to proclaim the death of God. The spiritual homeland to which Nietzsche wanted to go was too egoistic for Schweitzer. His hospital in Lambaréné for native people afflicted with leprosy, strangulated hernias, and other painful and life-threatening conditions was a repudiation of Nietzsche's vision. Both of these men had distinct responses to European spiritual decay, and saw what they thought was a better world. Nietzsche would enact that world through individual art and will to power. Schweitzer called upon service borne of the renunciation of the individual will, and a turning outward to aid the very people whom Nietzsche despised.

Christianity

Schweitzer's own Christianity and its central role in his viewpoint are complicated by other influences, such as Enlightenment reason and also Indian religions such as Buddhism and Jainism. His formulation of Christianity is complex enough to prompt scholars to ask if he indeed was a Christian. This question seems oddly absurd given his background as a practicing pastor and scholar who examined the "historical Jesus." In addition, he had an almost childlike appreciation of Jesus and saw his work in Africa as following Jesus. Yet Schweitzer was also a scholar of the New Testament and used his mind to examine in detail all that had been said about Jesus in scholarly works. So it is a blend of heart and head that Schweitzer brings to Jesus, adding the element of hand in his work in the hospital. Schweitzer combined three views of Jesus into one powerful holism: a critical-historical evaluation of the "historical Jesus"; a passionate and almost childlike following of him as a savior; and a spiritualized Jesus.

The Historical Jesus

Schweitzer's appreciation and following of Jesus comes from his religious background in childhood, but also too from his critical and intellectual examination of the "historical Jesus." This early work, *The Quest for the Historical Jesus*, is actually a synthesis of 67 authors and is his attempt to intellectually get to the core of the life and mission of Jesus of Nazareth. Schweitzer's deep passion for the message of Jesus of Nazareth combines with analysis to uncover its importance. This intellectual appreciation of Jesus is essential to Schweitzer's mature understanding of his mission.

He wanted to clear away, by critical and historical study of Jesus and many commentaries on his life, to his core message. The historical Jesus was all the more remarkable for Schweitzer, clad not in later theologies and interpretations, but revealed in his acts and deeds in a particular time of history. This Jesus served as the inspiration for Schweitzer, in all Jesus's passion and moral lessons, and to this Schweitzer, profoundly influenced by the Jesus of *Matthew* 10, added an apocalyptic eschatology.

Jesus's Core Message

Schweitzer's first step in discerning Jesus's core message is historical. He brackets through critical analysis the work of others, evaluating and showing how this work can help illuminate the life of Jesus. Schweitzer here sees Jesus preaching and enacting an ethic of love and a reverence for life; as Marvin Meyer notes: "For Schweitzer, then, Jesus becomes preeminently the proclaimer of love, and for Schweitzer Jesus becomes—like Schweitzer himself—the proclaimer of reverence for life."[17] For Schweitzer, Jesus's deeds and words are enough, without later theological and intellectual overlay. Schweitzer has ingeniously used his intellect to support what he believed in early life: the words and deeds of a man who captured his soul and intellect. As Jackson Lee Ice pointed out, Schweitzer had a strongly personal relationship with Jesus: "Schweitzer's attachment to Jesus, which is at times characterized by an almost childlike simplicity, seems incongruous with his scholarly views. He speaks of Jesus as the "master of our lives," the "Lord of our ethical wills," and "the one truly great man," and yet he finds him "a child of his age" whose late-Jewish apocalyptic vision of the Kingdom makes him "a stranger to our times"; who was in error about the consummation of history; and who suffered and died in disappointment."[18] This personal relationship sustained Schweitzer in his work, for he thought the message of Jesus triumphed over his disappointment and death. This message would later contribute to his formulation of Reverence for Life.

The Spiritualized Jesus

Ice points out that for all the work that Schweitzer did in reviewing the scholarship on Jesus in his historical quest, such historical detective work, though hermeneutically informed, does not reveal the essence of Jesus's life and message.[19] This essence must be gotten at through layers of cognitive exploration. Ice seems to take for granted that historians in fact do this in order to appreciate the life of a person. The work that Schweitzer did to evaluate the Jesus scholarship in his book indicates that this is far from universal. Schweitzer's work in uncovering the "historical" Jesus was fueled first and foremost by his deep appreciation of and allegiance to his life and deeds.

Schweitzer said that "Jesus has simply taken me prisoner since my childhood. . . . My going to Africa was an act of obedience to Jesus"[20] Thus his historical critical study of Jesus comes later and is secondary to his deep personal relationship that he had since childhood. Schweitzer's historical meta-analysis of Jesus was an attempt to get to the essence of Jesus's mission in his own time. Schweitzer very much believed that there is a diminishment when we try to see Jesus within our own worldview. As Oskar Kraus points out, when we do such interpretation, the worldview of Jesus "loses its primordial character and is no longer able to influence us in the same elemental way. That is the reason why the Jesus of modern theology is so strangely lifeless. When left in His own eschatological world, He is far greater and, in spite of His strangeness, affects us much more powerfully and elementally. . . . Actually He cannot be an authority for us on matters concerning knowledge, but solely on those concerning the will."[21]

This relationship remains, in greater importance than his critical-historical study of Jesus, and results in what he called a "practical eschatology," where what we do here in helping others is informed by directness and urgency. This is why too Schweitzer characterized his hospital at Lambaréné as "an outpost of the kingdom of God."[22] As Ara Paul Barsam succinctly states, Schweitzer "rejects all forms of spirituality that do not issue in action."[23] For Schweitzer this relationship with Jesus is "spiritualized" in that we know him through a direct relationship rather than critical-historical analysis and thus abstraction:

> No personality of the past can be transported to the present by means of . . . affirmations about His authoritative significance. We enter into relationship with Him only by being brought together in recognition of common will, and by experiencing a clarification, enrichment, and quickening of our will through His. Thus we find ourselves again in Him. In this sense every deeper relationship between humans partakes of a mystical quality.[24]

Schweitzer's deeply personal relationship with Jesus, though he recognized that it "partakes of a mystical quality," fueled commitment to his work.

In spite of his affirmation of Jesus as a figure of universal love and ethical deeds, Schweitzer agreed with Nietzsche's critique of modern Christianity, and believed it had lost its bearings. Schweitzer goes back to Old Testament prophets Amos and Isaiah, and to Zarathustra, to see that the ethical consists of being part of a social fabric, where one affirms the good in others and seeks to improve social conditions. He also saw this ethical action in the parable of Dives and Lazarus, which Schweitzer recounts in the beginning of his book *On the Edge of the Primeval Forest*.[25] Many of us have read Jesus's parable[26] about a rich man, commonly called Dives (Latin for "rich man") but unnamed in the parable, and a poor beggar, Lazarus. Dives lives a life of luxury while outside his home Lazarus lives destitute and covered with sores. The two die, Dives consigned to hell and Lazarus by the side of Abraham in heaven. When Dives pleads for mercy, Abraham admonishes him for not taking action in his lifetime. Dives cannot make up for what he did not do to help Lazarus in his own lifetime. It is actions here and now that matter in helping those in need.

This parable is part of Schweitzer's answer to the question he poses regarding how he came to where he was in late middle age: "I gave up my position of professor in the University of Strasbourg, my literary work, and my organ-playing, in order to go as a doctor to Equatorial Africa. How did that come about?"[27] He saw a great disparity between Europe and Africa, and believed the fruits of modern medical science as well as hard, committed labor could alleviate suffering in Africa. Many of us have done the same as Schweitzer, namely, reacted with concern and perhaps a vague plan to help when we hear about misery in a far off land, yet we have not been moved to action beyond perhaps a donation to a cause or a shared experience such as watching a telethon replete with prominent pop stars urging us to help. As Kraus notes, "The reason why Schweitzer's character seems so amazing to us lies in the fact that those actual ethical emotions which influenced his self-sacrificing decision would induce only a very small number of people to make a similar resolution."[28] His level of commitment, action, and determination against difficult odds is the testament to his character, where what is internally forged in one's own moral fiber as a pledge to serve others results in persistent ameliorative action.

Eastern Influences

Remarkably enough, given Schweitzer's unswerving allegiance to Jesus and the central role his Christian beliefs play in his life, there were other influences upon his thought that are outside Christianity, and that cause some to question whether in fact he was a Christian. Many of these influences come from Eastern thought and religion. What Schweitzer means by "ethical acceptance of the world" is that one accepts and affirms the world as is and one's part within it as interdependent. This is what he means by being ethical—to recognize this interdependence and affirm our need to do the good to keep Nature as robust and life-giving. It is not only to improve social conditions for humans, but to realize our own place within nature and to see the world through a pantheistic rather than anthropocentric lens.

Schweitzer got this in part from Spinoza, but more fundamentally from Indian thought, particularly Jainism, with its emphasis upon the divinity of all living things.[29] This Indian influence within European thought was recognized first in the work of Arthur Schopenhauer in the early nineteenth century. Ara Paul Barsam discusses how Schopenhauer and Schweitzer filtered Indian thought through European lenses. I will leave this fascinating discussion aside here, and focus more on the Indian influence Barsam and others note in Schweitzer's formulation of Reverence for Life. Though Schweitzer asserted he simply wanted to be a follower of Jesus, it was not only Christian or Western influences that led him to Reverence for Life as a guiding principle.

The idea of a boundless ethic came to Schweitzer from Indian sources. Barsam argues convincingly in an essay and later in a book for the importance of understanding the role that Indian thought played, particularly Jainism and its practice of ahimsā, characterized by nonviolence and noninjury in its dual aspects of respect for all life and compassion for life (karuna).[30] Finding evidence of Indian influences in Schweitzer's philosophy is not simply an intellectual exercise. Schweitzer's understanding of Reverence for Life went beyond human concerns; thus to attribute his idea of Reverence for Life to Goethe's idea of reverence in *Wilhelm Meister* as discussed in Chapter 2 is inaccurate. Goethe focused his reverence for those creatures that sustain human life. What sets Schweitzer apart is his pronouncement of a boundless ethic, and this is most clearly related to Jainism and ahimsā[31] even as Schweitzer connects this thought of a boundless ethic to the ethic of love he draws from the life and work of Jesus.

Schweitzer appreciated Schopenhauer for his emphasis on the elemental and central role of the will. Schopenhauer saw the will, or perhaps what we might call desire, as the elemental force in Nature, and what brings about misery and lack of fulfillment by its ceaseless striving. The way out for Schopenhauer is through a Buddhist negation of the will, and a separation of the will from its objects. Schweitzer also saw the ceaseless striving of the will as elemental, but with a different outcome from the negation that Schopenhauer saw this striving as issuing forth in action, though resignation and regret were also part of any action in the world for Schweitzer. For Schweitzer, a will to live, say, you as a human being, finds its source of value and efficacy not wholly within itself but in relation to others, other "wills" to live. That is why Schweitzer saw all life as sacred. Barsam notes the clarity with which Schweitzer realized this insight by quoting him twice on this point:

> The ethics of reverence for life makes no distinction between higher and lower, more precious and less precious lives. . . . How can we know the importance other living organisms have in themselves and in terms of the universe?[32]
>
> And I'll be damned if I recognize any *objectively valid* distinctions in life. Every life is sacred! Value judgments are made out of subjective necessity, but they have no validity beyond that. The proposition that every life is sacred is absolute. In this respect I will always remain a heretic. It is a question of principle, one that reaches deep into the foundation of my outlook on life.[33]

Here Schweitzer is affirming the boundless ethic of his idea of Reverence for Life that links him not to his much-admired mentor Goethe, but to Indian thought, particularly the Jain doctrine of ahimsā.

A Creative Tension

For some commentators, Schweitzer vacillates between theism and pantheism. This is not a problem for Schweitzer, but a creative tension and "unsolved conflict" between philosophy and religion. Here he replies at length in a letter on January 2, 1924, to Oskar Kraus's concern about this supposed vacillation:

> Hitherto it has been my principle never to express in my philosophy more than I have experienced as a result of absolutely logical reflection. That is why I never speak in philosophy of "God" but only of the "universal will-to-live," which I realize in my consciousness in a twofold way: firstly, as a creative will outside myself and secondly, as an ethical will within me. . . . That is why I prefer to content myself with a description of the experience of reflection, leaving pantheism and theism as an unsolved conflict in my soul. But if I speak the traditional language of religion, I use the word "God" in its historical definiteness and indefiniteness, just as I speak in ethics of 'Love' in place of "Reverence for Life." For I am anxious to impart to others my inwardly experienced thought in all its original vividness and in its relationship to traditional religion.[34]

Schweitzer realizes that he can only go so far with philosophical reflection, and that he cannot come to any definite answer via this means, but can only give a "description of the experience of reflection." The language of religion is appropriate when speaking about its experiences, as Schweitzer notes in the final paragraph, as these experiences are elemental for him, and religious experience has a primacy in his outlook. This relationship and conflict between philosophical reflection and religious conviction plays out in the context of the development of the most important personal relationship of his life, with his wife Hélène, his partner and soul mate. He searched and finally found his mission in life at least partly through her.

3

An Evolving Relationship: Albert and Hélène

One of the new places to get information and insight into Schweitzer's motivation comes in recently translated and published letters that he exchanged with his future wife, Hélène Bresslau.[1] It is not easy interpreting any such relationship, so I will tread lightly in any pronouncements or attempts at analysis of the psychology of a century-old courtship and eventual marriage. My contention in this chapter is simple, that Albert Schweitzer developed an unsure and inchoate ideal to a resolved course of action by sounding these ideas in correspondence with his future wife. What is the effect of Hélène upon Albert, and what was the map of his decision to go to Africa, and how did this develop? These questions all touch upon human growth, development, reflection, and maturity, and thus are educational issues in a broad sense. The answer to these questions comes at least in part from the letters that Schweitzer and his future wife exchanged during their long courtship.

A Courtship through Letters

These letters have been recently compiled by their only child, Rhena Schweitzer Miller, and help to answer questions about how Schweitzer's motivation to go to Africa developed over time, and how it mirrored the growth of a bond between him and Hélène, and what needs were satisfied or at least addressed by his commitment to work in Africa and by his marriage. But perhaps just as importantly, these letters give us a better understanding of Hélène Bresslau and what role she played in Schweitzer's moral development, as well as her own thoughts and ideas. We may think too about the role of other people or a particular other person may have in the development of a strong character in a person. Hélène was critical in the development of Schweitzer's character and his own movement from a sense of wanting to help, to the man of action that he became when the two of them embarked to Africa. Rhena Schweitzer Miller discusses this in the introduction to the collection: "These letters also throw a new light on my father's intellectual development and the slow ripening of his decision to go to Africa. The young man who knew what he wanted but not how it could be attained became the man of action who knew his path."[2] The daughter of Albert and Hélène does not directly affirm the role of her mother in her father's thought here, but just acknowledges the fact that the development of his decision from an ideal to action and deed ripened and took hold of him in a potent way through the letters the two exchanged over a long period of time and separation. Hélène's own story is a bittersweet one, as her health did not allow her to spend time with him in Africa. She lived in Europe most of her life, and raised Rhena, seeing her husband when he would come for visits to Europe.

We may need to adjust our cultural lenses here too to understand how the relationship developed over this extended period of years from a friendship shared over common ideals to a marriage. More can be said about their relationship than James Brabazon's valid though insufficient comment: "(I)t was not a love-match, at least not on his side. It was an arrangement by which two people, both dedicated to a single cause, could work together."[3] First of all, it was conducted long distance, by letters, for many years. Far from hiding their feelings and emotions, Albert and Hélène funneled such into writing to each other in often passionate and anguished letters. Writing down one's thoughts and emotions can be both revealing and concealing, and any reader of another's letters must assume that they were not meant to be read by others. It was a lengthy courtship, and we can look to these letters to see ways that we, as readers now a century on, can listen and hear what is being said. It is unusual to have a written, formal record of such thoughts these days. Those of us who have taught online may have used "threaded" conversations in chat rooms, and you can follow a line of thought in a blog and its comments. But letters composed deliberately are not as much a part of our culture anymore. We may write someone a letter, but we do not exchange letters over a long period of time, nor do we save these so we can look at them whole and as dialogue.

Letters and Diaries

Diaries may be comparable to the intensity and seriousness that Albert Schweitzer and Héléne Bresslau exhibited in their correspondence. A diary can be an interior dialogue or the diary itself can serve as a person with whom one corresponds, such as the examples of the diaries of Anne Frank and Etty Hillesum, a Dutch teenager and a Dutch woman who were killed in Nazi concentration camps in World War II. Schweitzer did not use his letters as conscious means toward transformation quite in the ways that Hillesum and Frank did with their diaries, but we see the transformation over time that did occur with these three examples. Anne Frank, as a thirteen-year-old girl starting a diary, treated it as a "living person with whom she corresponded,"[4] as well as a place to compose letters to her friends. Hillesum used her diary in resistance to anti-Semitism but also, as David T. Hansen describes, the diary became a transformative instrument that enabled her spiritual journey.[5]

I shall have more to say in the final chapter about Hansen's idea of "tenacious humility" that he notes in Hillesum's diary, but for now suffice it to say that both the young girl Frank and the young woman Hillesum wrote in their diaries not only as a means to control the chaos and terror that, finally, engulfed and killed them, but as interior spiritual and personal transformation. The letters Albert Schweitzer and Hélène Bresslau exchanged were in calmer circumstances, but were no less transformative for Albert at least. We can only guess what would have become of the Dutch woman Hillesum and the Dutch teenager Frank had they not been killed in Nazi concentration camps. We can see what became of the work of Albert Schweitzer and Hélène Bresslau, foreshadowed with increasing clarity in the letters they exchanged prior to marriage. Schweitzer reached out to Bresslau and in so doing was able to see more clearly the path that his life would take, though neither of them could have foreseen that she would not be able to tolerate the difficult climate of Lambaréné, likened to me by a visitor as living in a steam room. Hélène returned to Europe and lived there, seeing Albert regularly but usually only when he traveled back for visits, fund raising, or speaking engagements.

Character and resolve revealed

We can see a fuller picture of Schweitzer's character through examining the early development of this relationship in these letters. To take an unusual and demanding path to one's lifework can help us decipher one's character traits, especially if one documents the evolution of the decision the way that Albert and Hélène did in their letters and the way he did in his autobiographical writings. In this sense, Schweitzer's resolve is both immediate, and developed over time through mediation in his work and his relationship with Hélène. By using their letters and comparing them to his own autobiographical work, one can see a fuller picture of this resolve as part of his mature character. Schweitzer was a private man who did not allow his feelings to show to others in any great degree. So, these letters let us have a portal into some of his thoughts as he and his future wife both develop a relationship that turns into a marriage, and decide upon the focus of his life's work, as well as leave behind a promising career. Hélène played a crucial role in Albert's life as confidante and in determining more exactly why they went to Africa. I am fortunate in my interpretation to draw upon personal insight gained in telephone and face-to-face conversation and my own written correspondence with their only child, Rhena Schweitzer Miller.

The tone is set in the first letters of the collection. Here Albert is busy with work and apologetic to Hélène, and the letters themselves are short. Her letter is longer and reveals her anguish, longing, and dependence: "To be sure, I do not yet know my way—it is much easier for a man whose profession gives him direction—will you help me to find mine?"[6]

Schweitzer, in writing back to her, is also unsure of present circumstances, while knowing that a direction for both will come forth, that it is like a "needle of the compass until it finds the pole. *We will find it.*"[7] He sees Hélène as someone who will nurture and support him in what he thinks now is their common quest. Yet, what he does not see or realize is *her* anguish and *her own* restless spirit. His own solution for her restlessness appears in a subsequent letter in talking about how nature gives in, as he says, after two stormy days. He strongly identifies nature with woman and the struggle for identity, and sets up the dichotomy of his call to be in obedience to Jesus, whereas for her the call is of the heart.[8]

While he may mean to console Bresslau, his words are probably more than a little unsettling: "This is how women struggle until they accept their fate, and then comes fall, smiling, when all charms and richness, which they hide inside, unfold—knowing through struggles."[9] At once, he characterizes women as searching through interior struggles, but then draws upon her in his own struggle for identity: "This is my dream—to educate ministers and to be in daily contact with them, not just an office-pastor relation, but a human-pastor-idealist exchange,"[10] and goes so far as to see the Enlightenment philosopher Immanuel Kant as his Christmas friend, thus joining Kant's rationality and sense of duty to the sacred Christian holiday.

Schweitzer wanted to teach and influence others, but found himself trapped in the thick of petty jealousies and politics at the seminary. He had a vision of what he wanted to do, but the more these ideas came into fruition and became real the more engaged he was with Hélène. He slowly came to realize that she was his soul mate and companion. Even books he read reminded him of this debt he was incurring to her. While reading a book by Elisabeth von Heyking, he says: "I trembled when I read the sentence in which she says that a man owns what he has seen, felt, and thought to another being who has awakened what had been slumbering in him."[11] Unfortunately, here and at other crucial places in the exchange, we have no response from Hélène.

The slumber and potentiality Schweitzer felt was a source of restlessness. He wanted to act, and found that his life as a musician, pastor, and professor did not provide outlets for what was churning within him. His comments about Friedrich Nietzsche show what he thought of a life of relentless thinking that did not result in action. Reflecting upon Nietzsche's book *Beyond Good and Evil,* Schweitzer saw the author as being entirely too inward and focused on egoistic needs. Nietzsche did not come out of his cage, but tore himself to pieces in the end because he could not focus his energies outward toward action.[12] For Schweitzer, the primacy of action over inwardly focused, self destructive, mere thought is capsulated in this dictum: "I believe because I act."[13]

Connecting action to belief was, of course, to be his lifelong theme, integral to his identity and to his educational legacy. He was searching for a way to not only *be* in the world but *do* for it. Working as a professor, or even as a musician, did not satisfy this need, as he tells Hélène:

> I feel as if my whole life is an immense dream: People around me do not understand me anymore; they suspect something that they do not know; they cannot understand that I feel removed and especially why I don't care about my "career" as professor! As if that would be my goal, the career of a professor!—No, I want to "*live*," live my life—you understand me![14]

For Schweitzer, the way beyond professorial activity to a place and station where he could connect his belief to action is filtered through the layers of his deep Christian faith. In these letters, he reveals just how deeply he wrestled with a faith that had been so much a part of his upbringing. He uses his Christian faith as a subject of his questions, and sees such questioning as key to the development of his thinking.[15] Schweitzer experiences the *ennui* and spiritual exhaustion of the era. The hypocrisy that Schweitzer believed was in the fabric of the culture prompted a radical reexamination of his own stance toward his faith, to the point where he considered that Jesus died an atheist because "Did He not say when He faced death, 'My God, my God, why have you forsaken me?'"[16] Schweitzer saw that courage was needed to face such a radical and disturbing thought, but he wondered if there were others of his faith who were willing to think so. He was restive and felt trapped, and did not see courageous thought in those with whom he worked, but rather rote, accepted learning that did not prod him or others to strive higher. Hélène repeatedly comes to his rescue as she tries to prevent his despair. Her example of independence helps him to clarify his motives. She reasons that to be a real Christian is to love Jesus Christ, and to not be taken in by trappings and formalities.[17] These formalities of organized religion are merely nominal, and this naming shrouds the phenomenon of this core belief. Hélène mirrors for Schweitzer his own struggles, while at the same time transforming them for him and helping him on his way.

We now too begin to see what Hélène became for Albert. She reveals that the exchange of letters meant even more to him than sharing intellectual ideas, as above all, she was a trusted listener and confidante.[18] But she helped him too in moments of doubt: "You help me, you push me ahead."[19] Even given all of this contact and weaving together of their experiences, he still could not see that they should become man and wife, and suggested even that she marry another.[20]

This exclamation for what he desired for her future could not have been what she wanted to hear, though we do not have her immediate response. Several months later, Schweitzer writes the most revealing of the letters regarding how he feels about Hélène. It is near her thirtieth birthday on the day of December 21st that he usually celebrates with his aunt, reliving the holiday ritual of discussing Immanuel Kant and lighting some pine boughs in the fireplace. For his aunt, Schweitzer has had "this deep affection, the first in my life."[21] Now he has shifted his attention to Hélène, and wants to make her part of this December 21st ritual, even to replace his cherished aunt. He celebrates it alone in his mind, with the images of the fire, his work on Kant, and now Hélène. He wonders about the present and future course of his life while his mind is racing.

> I don't want to be an overworked, egotistical workhorse. With 30 years I begin a new life! What will I have in store for me? . . . How can I possibly find fulfillment in my life? I have the desire to give, to give what I have in me and to improve through great and selfless action—and sometimes I smile when I see that people imagine that I have only one great wish: to become a "full professor"! . . . I hardly dare to read the journals of the French Missionary Society, Sister Hélène, noble soul! Because every time I open one of them, I read "We need people! Are there none?" And then I tell myself that it is easy to substitute the head of a seminary, an assistant professor, also the vicar and the organist for the concerts at Wilhelm's Kirche—but there I will be needed. Let us wait: how this spirit of life, this mysterious Being that we call God will lead and guide me, the heretic priest.[22]

Schweitzer sees his previous life, up until age 30, marked by "pale"[23] achievements of scholarship and music. Action is now necessary to give the color and energy of life to his work: "I have given up the ambition to become a great scholar, I want to be more—*simply a human*"[24] and "But I want to free myself from this bourgeois life that would kill everything in me; I want to live, I want to do something as a disciple of Jesus."[25] He was involved in learning about others, and wanted to be and act as someone. His teacher, the great organist Charles-Marie Widor, had admonished him, "The general does not go to the front with a rifle,"[26] but Schweitzer had firmly decided his life's course. Music and scholarship, though he would not cease activity in these areas, would not be enough to satisfy his restless spirit.

The year 1905 would be crucial for Albert and Hélène, as he decides how to make the decision of what to do with the rest of his life. He envies Hélène for finding a way to a "great task"[27] of studying to be a nurse while he is "simply a privatdocent—a human who lectures, who does not act."[28] Indeed, any efforts toward action even in his professorial role are looked upon by others with suspicion, as he reveals,[29] when his colleagues do not approve of his mentoring of students. His chafing at the expected role of the privatdocent here is palpable, and he tries to convey it to Hélène, though he comes to realize that a new life awaits him at age 30.[30] Indeed, in talking about the lessons he is teaching the children, he states that there are lessons he himself is learning, but not just from books that he can recite, but those in his heart that he could learn, and be part of his heart.[31]

Letters from 1905 are incandescent in their emotional intensity as he searches for answers to what to do next. Schweitzer is really struggling with his decision to continue his work. He worries about the amount of time he is spending with his students, and is admonished by his colleagues and supervisor for this commitment. When he contemplates becoming the successor of Knittel, he confesses to Hélène: "I am suffocating."[32] Clearly Schweitzer is in a spiritual crisis and seems determined to follow a path that will lead him away from a respectable, bourgeois career as a pastor and scholar. He doesn't just want to limit himself to be only a professor, but he wants to follow in the path of serving Jesus.[33] He comes to this realization with Hélène, and tells her she is the only person to whom he can be judged, and it is her strength that envelopes him.[34]

She too derives strength from him though she clearly displays more anguish at this: "There was a fear I had the other day when I said, 'Leave me lying by the roadside,'—because I was afraid to see the fear and worry in your face that my complaints had caused."[35] Hélène shares with him information about their increasing interest in conditions of the Congo, and the atrocities that were committed there: "I told my parents about this evening, and for the first time, mentioned the Congo to them. I wrote that if the description of the atrocities is based on fact, no responsible person could remain a calm observer."[36] Hélène thinks of his communication with the Paris Missionary Society and how that may transform his life and her own.

In October 1905, Schweitzer finally receives the word from the Paris Missionary Society that he has awaited, and learns that he will be called into service by the society in two years.[37] The calm that can accompany the finality of a long discussed and debated decision comes to him. At once it was a straightforward decision that he saw as reverberating among souls. He saw in the simplicity of those who served in the Congo something that was missing for him, for it was a pureness of motive and spirit that he did not see in his daily life as a minister. It even leads to a transformation of how he views his Christian faith: "What has this child done to our lives—no, not the child, but the man!!"[38] Here is a distinction between Jesus as son of God and Jesus as the man who committed himself to service and, importantly, toward a freedom derived from an active ministry. He is relieved that he made this choice, this momentous decision to change the course of his life.

The resolution to act in this manner was complicated for Schweitzer of course. For one, it was simple with the pure motive that he didn't doubt, he had clear and powerful anguish that needed to be dealt with, and it seemed that this abstract idea of helping others in dire need would do the trick. But he had no more than this vague idea of a calling. His family and others are there as he reflects, but as we shall find out, they are opposed to the trip and wonder about his emotional state, while many of his colleagues in his professions think his change of direction in life toward service in Africa is ill advised.

He later talks about how he is giving up his dream of being an educator of the ministry. But it is an education of a different sort that he would be about to embark upon. What he means by being a different kind of educator is to go against the rote and regimented learning that he himself experienced, such as when he was chastised for not remembering minute trivia about Homer's epics. He rather tries to enlighten his students about happiness, about how they as youth must take advantage of what comes to them, but they are baffled by him.[39] He is not heard by his students or by his colleagues, and believes it is only Hélène who hears what he is about. He comes to his decision but only after bouncing the idea off her for feedback and counsel.

Hélène helps him to finally make the decision, and he shares his thoughts with her about her abiding support and influence: "I think of you as somebody, as the only person who has the right to judge me. The powers of your thinking envelopes me, protects me, and sustains me."[40] Schweitzer wants to share this with her when he finally receives an answer from the Paris mission, and reports this in a remarkable letter that befits the occasion, at the end of August 1905. At once he focuses on simplicity of thought, as what had crystallized for him, partly due to his restlessness with teaching that complicated methods removed from direct experience, and his desire to serve. He saw in the straightforwardness of those who served in the Congo something that was missing in his life—a purity of motive and spirit that he did not experience as a pastor, professor, or musician.

For Schweitzer, the clarity of his mission gave him strength. He is relieved to finally commit himself, and to leave behind what for him had become an anguished and abstract sense of what to do next. He continues to reflect, and these reflections and working out of his thoughts he does most comfortably with Hélène and in these letters.

After the momentous year of 1905, Hélène shares birthday greetings with him in January 1906, underscoring what would mark their union: a regard for the well-being of others: "My friend, happy birthday from the depths of my heart!—And yet a wish for happiness? Only as we understand it, *the happiness of those who do not strive for their own, at least not the happiness of those who pursue only their own.*"[41] But this well-being, increasingly for Schweitzer, does not come from teaching, or even mentoring students, from being what he considers a bourgeois European intellectual in a dying and sick culture. It will not come from time in Europe, but to a commitment in a far off land: "I feel and know that here I would never become the one I meant to be, a human who plunges into life and gives everything he has in him, whatever his lot may be."[42] But it is only with Hélène that he is able to share these ideas. His parents, particularly his mother, do not approve, and he has conflicts with them over his chosen work. His mother wants to know why he seeks fulfillment elsewhere and what is there for him.[43] He shares his yearning with Hélène; the constant striving that informs his faith: "We know that Christianity is a constantly creative spirit, a spirit that remains itself only through constant work."[44] Yet Schweitzer is also matter-of-fact about what he has decided will be his life work. He remarks to Hélène that his negotiations with the Paris Missionary Society, though momentous for him and for her, were "almost like a contract with a publisher."[45] At once it was a simple decision that he saw as reverberating among souls.

What Schweitzer saw in the work of those missionaries in the Congo may have been too simple, but it sufficed for him. He was caught in what he considered a "suffocating" and predictable life of hollow service as a bourgeois minister, writer, and musician. What stands out in these letters is how we see his constantly evolving development of motivation to go to Africa, to work as a missionary doctor and to leave behind the life he had in Europe. The value of the letters for our understanding is to see how he reveals this slowly to Hélène, and how this resolve becomes clearer to him too. He discovers the wellspring of motivation within himself by sharing these ideas with her. She listens and he shares with her.[46] However this relationship through letters and infrequent meetings is almost wholly one-sided. It is his Aunt Tata who states to him what was becoming increasingly apparent: "I have lived with you long enough to know that the woman who will share your life will suffer often and deeply by being bound to a human being who is so engrossed in his work and his thoughts. . . . She will have to give up a great deal, your H. B."[47] The letter is remarkable in its admission of the care and attention that Schweitzer felt for Hélène. He realizes, through what another close woman has said to him, the burden of sacrifice this one must give to him. It is not so much a warning as an admission of what he sees to come in his life. We can ask at this point if Hélène come to accept this course in life and will their relationship develop over time?

While 1905 may have been the time when Schweitzer came to his decision, this next year is a time to confirm it. Hélène sends him a birthday greeting to follow his own road. Their birthday wishes are all so imbued with a sense of mission and common purpose, so different than what one may get with a birthday greeting today. They shared a deep commitment toward a mission in a complete and passionate way: Again, in contrast to his pale and unsatisfying life at the seminary, he writes: "I feel and know that here I would never become the one I meant to be, a human who plunges into life and gives everything he has in him, whatever his lot may be."[48] He discovers the source of motivation within himself and reveals this transformation in the letters, slowly not only to Hélène, but to himself.[49] He receives some encouragement from friends, such as the conductor Ochs, who understands the depth of Schweitzer's feelings and motivations, but his family and many of his other friends continue to be baffled and disappointed by his chosen path in life.

Schweitzer continues with his explorations, and the letters of 1906 take on a more introspective quality, where we can see him struggling with deciding what is God.[50] He asks himself repeatedly, "What is God, Something infinite in which we rest. But it is not a personality; it becomes a personality only in us. The spirit of the world that in man comes to the consciousness of himself" and clearly he sees Hélène as his soul mate, the one who bucks him up when he feels spiritual depletion. She realizes that he has taken on a great deal, too, and worries about him, but is not above slightly chiding him: "How are things at the hospital? My great one will not seriously despair if he doesn't succeed just as he wants in everything immediately on the second day, will he?"[51] Hélène is not so taken with "My Great One" as she teasingly calls him. She does admire him for the stamina he exhibits[52] and laments, "You see, Bery—I don't know if you can understand this—I have such an unquenchable need for rest."[53]

This spirit keeps him going through times of exhaustion. As 1906 ends, Hélène and Albert have accomplished a great deal of the inward work of their spiritual and emotional understanding of the commitment to serve others, and Albert has overcome some doubts with her help and strengthened his resolve. He knows now the path he will take, what will turn out to be his life work. Hélène has accepted his decision, and indeed encouraged him. As 1907 begins, Schweitzer sees most clearly how they will develop their life-long partnership. They fall into a pattern of familiarity. He complains of exhaustion, while she admonishes him for being so driven. He has cemented his bond with Hélène, and strengthened his determination to carry out a life of service. She is the support for what he wants to do, and affirms him in ways that his family and friends do not.

Schweitzer still sees their relationship as a friendship, deepened of course by their devotion to a common ideal. This relationship gives him pleasure, "the only happiness in my life."[54] He says that his duty is on par with this friendship, but Schweitzer seems incapable of seeing his relationship with Hélène as anything more than serious and dutiful. He is "proud" of her, seemingly a detached approbation for a couple who will eventually marry, and he demands of her the same exacting behavior he himself exhibits.

But 1909 is the year when their lives would change dramatically. He finishes his studies, and they discuss embarking to Africa. He signals this further development in their relationship as they move closer to its defining stage by stating, after a performance of Wagner's *Parsifal*, that he realizes what "knowing through compassion" means beyond how it is presented in the opera.[55] The emotions become more intense and more heartfelt. Schweitzer realizes what kind of sacrifice he has asked of himself, and also of Hélène much more has he asked:

> And all these years of waiting you have sacrificed for me—almost ten! The most beautiful years of your life in which you could have had all the happiness that life has to offer for a woman—house, hearth, happiness, children—you have led a life of hard work, shaken by struggles with yourself and your family, full of sadness . . . with much heavy loneliness . . . and all that for me![56]

Yet Hélène has become inextricably part of the decision that he has made. He clearly sees her as a partner in the sacrifice and the duty-bound commitment.

But it is a commitment that expresses itself at once in an uncomplicated way: to be simply human means one's life will be simple and to stand in simple faith.[57] It is a common belief that they share, or at least he characterizes it as so, though he was the one who developed the idea and shared it with her. At the end of 1911, Albert writes a letter to Hélène's parents, proposing marriage and that she accompany him to the Congo. He realizes that this request is extraordinary: "Ever since this plan became a reality in me, I have felt a pain when I look at you and know about the sacrifice I have to ask from you."[58]

Here in the letters Schweitzer has been able to reveal himself personally, in the conflicts that he had and in the development of his commitment over time. While it is beyond the scope of this book to explore the effect Hélène had upon Albert in greater detail, we can see in their relationship ways in which it will influence his thought later, especially on educational matters. Clearly what is apparent in the correspondence of this intense, earnest, and disillusioned scholar now embarking on a life of medical service is a passionate commitment that leads to personal sacrifice, which is shared with his future wife, though not equally. He now is committed to action.

Coda: Rhena

Not only would Albert spend long periods of time away from his wife, but also their only child, Rhena Schweitzer, who was born on his forty-fourth birthday. Rhena compiled the letters I have drawn upon in this chapter, and she provides further insight into her parents.

I interviewed Mrs. Miller (1919–2009) twice in March 2005 at the home she shared with her daughter and family, high atop a mountain overlooking the ocean in Pacific Palisades, California. Though she shared her father's birthday, she had seemingly little else as a common experience with him as she grew up in Europe with her mother. Rhena was thrust into taking care of the hospital, with little experience in this area, when her father was dying. Later, Rhena supported the work of her father by disseminating his ideas and speaking at conferences and workshops. She attended conferences at the Schweitzer institutes at Chapman University in 2001 and at Quinnipiac University in 2005.

I began a correspondence with Rhena several years before meeting her at her home in California in 2005. Though she had not met me, she responded promptly and warmly to my letters. I had gone out to California to spend time with her while also on a research trip to the Albert Schweitzer Institute at Chapman University. At the time she was 86, and I sensed I would have few opportunities to hear her perceptions of her father and especially what she saw as a relation of his work to education. I drove to Chapman University after checking into my hotel in Los Angeles. There I was greeted by Marvin Meyer, the director of the Schweitzer Institute, and a renowned Biblical scholar. We ate lunch in the sunshine at a small café across from the university. Meyer let me consult the Schweitzer archives and make photocopies of some of the Schweitzer memorabilia in the Institute. I particularly wanted copies of some pictures of Schweitzer I had not seen elsewhere.

Meyer prepared me for my meeting with Rhena, saying that she was warm and open, and eager to meet me. I had found that to be the case when I spoke to her on the telephone to arrange the visit. She insisted on giving me explicit directions to where she lived. At the time, I was unaware of where exactly it was, or that she lived in a small apartment on the grounds of her daughter's home, the pianist and medical doctor Christiane Engel. Rhena told me to come that evening for a concert that Christiane and the Stern Quartet were to give for friends and family.

Sunset Boulevard shifts in landscape and composition as it makes its way through Los Angeles, West Hollywood, Beverly Hills, and finally through Brentwood and Pacific Palisades to the ocean. I was convinced that it would be easy to find the home, as I had little difficulty finding my way around the well-marked streets and freeways of southern California. It was not so. I drove past the entrance to the street several times, until I finally entered it correctly. Rhena had given me the right directions; I just could not find the turnoff. Heading up the street on a steep incline directly off Sunset in Pacific Palisades, I was again confronted by the unexpected. It was getting dark, and I kept climbing, past gated driveways, on a winding road to a mountaintop, overlooking the ocean to the west. Finally, I came to the home, and entered with the concert about to begin. I quietly said hello to Rhena, who was seated alone at a dining table toward the back, and then the music started. The Stern Quartet, with Christiane on the piano, played Mozart. I chatted and ate after the concert with the friends and neighbors, and exchanged a few introductory pleasantries with Rhena. I left feeling that I had been greeted with hospitality and interest, and I was excited for our regularly scheduled visit and conversation the next day.

When I arrived back, Christiane greeted me and pointed out spots of interest in the spectacular ocean view from the deck of the house. Rhena was down in her apartment, and I was to go see her there. The apartment was a small house, just a kitchen, bathroom, and combination living area and bedroom, down a steep flight of stairs from the main home where the concert had been the night before. The main room was large, split by a divider to separate living and sleeping areas. In the divider was a bookshelf and at the end of it, a large bust of her father Albert Schweitzer. It was here that we sat, drank tea, and discussed her view of her father's legacy for education. Rhena was lucid and spoke vividly from memory of her childhood education. She was particularly passionate about the influence of the "Herrenhüter" (Moravian Brethren) upon her father's thinking, and their influence on her as teachers. Her father remembered a simple Christian piety and way of life, and wanted his daughter to absorb that:

> In the intervals of his tours across Europe, Schweitzer established a new base for himself and his family at Königsfeld in the Black Forest. The health of his wife required altitude and he built a story-and-a-half house at the edge of a peaceful village, dominated by the presence of the Moravian Brethren (*Herrenhüter*) who had a retreat there. From his earliest youth, Schweitzer had felt drawn to the Brethren with their simple Christian spirit, even as he felt drawn toward the friends, and he wanted his daughter, Rhena—now three—to grow up among them and to attend their school. He himself established close personal relations with many of the Brethren.[59]

Rhena didn't speak of the nature of the curriculum or what she learned, but rather focused on the unassuming and caring nature of the brethren. It obviously made an indelible impression upon her so that she recalled their influence 80 years later. She remembered being taught with forthright directness by the brethren.

As she spoke with obvious joy about this experience with the Herrenhüter, I thought of teaching history and philosophy to prospective teachers at my university. I discuss the Moravian bishop and educator Johann Amos Comenius in one class, but I didn't say more than that he championed universal education and was an inspiration for the founding fathers of America's early republic—men like Jefferson who recalled Comenius's work as they planned their great experiment. Comenius was more than that, as I found out later. The great educator of the seventeenth century was part of the Moravian Brethren order. In addition to championing universal education, he proposed an idea of stages of development and what we now call age-appropriate instruction.[60] However, these pedagogical theories and methods were instrumental to the end point of instruction for Comenius: piety, and appreciation where the idea of universal education through stages of development occurs. The means toward this piety was universal knowledge that he laid out with fervor in his chief work, *The Great Didactic*.

Rhena simply had noted that her own time with the Herrenhüter and their example of teaching and caring formed her own ideals of education. I wish I had taken more time to speak to Rhena about this at that point, as I had no other occasion to do so. I would have wanted to know what the school was like, whether her father ever talked to her in any depth about what she learned from the brethren, and how instruction, and more importantly, their example of pious living, had affected her later in life. We continued to drink tea, sitting at a modest table a few feet from a large bust of her father, and talked for a few hours. And then it was time to go to the main house.

Rhena and I climbed up the stairs, and with my cheap camera I snapped her as she rose out of the ground to the level of the house. She scolded me good naturedly for taking this picture. The picture I took reminded me of those pictures of her father sawing the *okoumé* wood to remake his hospital, and tending to other manual tasks. He did many things himself, simply and without fanfare, and I could see that his daughter took after him. I recalled the anecdote about Harry S. Truman, who when asked what he did after he stepped down as president, stated that he took the luggage and put it in the attic. I said goodbye to Rhena, thinking that I would not see her again, though I did briefly at the conference in her father's name that autumn at Quinnipiac University. There we again chatted, at the reception for the keynote speaker, Jane Goodall, but the next day Rhena had a health emergency and was unable to participate in a panel discussion. I spoke to her on the telephone a few times after that, and she was pleased with what I showed her of this book. I wish I had completed it before she died.

Image 3.1   Photograph of Rhena Miller and the author

4

To Africa: From Thought to Conviction and Action

Albert Schweitzer and Hélène Bresslau spent years in a slowly developing relationship where he began to see more clearly in the loving exchanges he had with her the path that his life would take. Schweitzer's solidifying of resolve was deceptively simple and shrouded by passing years. Can we learn, from his fateful decision to go to Africa, about the kinds of decisions made by teachers and other educators, as they commit themselves to a life of service? A close colleague of mine quipped once that we are teachers because we didn't want to go the extreme route of becoming missionaries. This casual remark has meaning in this context, for the continuum of decisions made by educators about their work links the missionary zeal at one end to the more measured and ordinary decision to teach made by students in education programs at colleges and universities every year. Schweitzer's decision to make Africa his destination was a radical one. Though the decision making is similar to that of one deciding to teach, such decisions by prospective teachers are not usually as extreme as that of Schweitzer, except in unusual circumstances.

A Momentous Decision

As Schweitzer reflected when he and Hélène were about to go to Lambaréné, what appealed to him about being a doctor there was that he could just act. He assured his sponsor, the Paris Missionary Society, whose leaders were concerned about his unorthodox religious writings, that he would not preach. In fact, he planned on being "dumb as a carp."[1] However, several months after arriving in Africa, Schweitzer was invited to take part in the preaching by the missionaries there. To his great delight, he found they shared a "piety of obedience to Jesus," and a practical approach to simple Christian activity, quite free from the dogma and misgivings of the Missionary Society's committee in Paris.

The narrative already established is that Schweitzer decided to leave his scholarly and artistic life at age 30 and devote himself to service. He sought salvation through his work due to a deep concern for what he thought was a decaying European culture. Schweitzer parted company with the pessimistic writings of Spengler and Nietzsche, making committed action his means of cultural and spiritual regeneration. He often said that he wanted to make his life his argument. Such a decision has moral importance, whether it be extreme as with Schweitzer, or less so. For Schweitzer, it was a turn toward action and to others, away from the scholarly life as he had experienced it. Education here is simply not just acquisition of knowledge, but a passionate commitment of the person toward a specific path and goal, that of service toward others.

Though Schweitzer's decision to leave a promising academic and artistic career in Europe appears sudden, it was not. Though it was a momentous decision that affected his life and that of others profoundly, the biographical evidence, especially letters that Schweitzer exchanged with his future wife, Hélène Bresslau, discussed in the previous chapter, builds the case that this fateful decision grew in depth and commitment over time and with the aid of dialogue and loving struggle. Schweitzer decided to lead a life devoted to others in Africa, far in distance and environment from where he grew up and made his initial reputation, and, as it turned out, away from his wife, Hélène, and daughter, Rhena, for all but the initial years.

A Call to Serve

Clearly, Schweitzer's desire for knowledge and to put it into action was at odds with the kind of teaching that he received and that he was expected to give. He saw something beyond the everyday teaching and learning of lessons. He heard what could be termed a "call" to serve. This call for service has been discussed in detail by the educational philosopher David T. Hansen. In *The Call to Teach*,[2] Hansen argues that for some people teaching is a vocation or calling, which he describes as "a form of public service that yields enduring personal fulfillment to those who provide it."[3] While Hansen is determined not to make teaching so extraordinary that it is only something practiced by the few, he deals with the issue of imitation or inspiration by someone such as Schweitzer: "Far from denoting something esoteric, restricted to an enlightened or heroic few, the idea of teaching as a vocation calls attention to the personal and service-oriented dimensions of the practice that draw people to it, and that enable them to find success despite adversity and difficulty."[4] This kind of service is not necessarily heroic or extraordinary, though of course it can be.

While it is certainly the case that there are many great and even more good and dedicated teachers, this happy fact does not preclude the inspiration afforded by someone like Schweitzer. In fact, it may be just that this view of Hansen, so necessary to understand a certain type of vocation or calling, has prevented us from seeing what can be the contributions of Schweitzer's educational efforts. For if we are to only see Schweitzer as the legend then we cannot see what the concrete contributions from both his thinking and his practice might be. Thus I am approaching vocation from a slightly different angle than Hansen. I want to pull away the shroud around Schweitzer, and show that what he did has practical import, but that his example in its extraordinariness and mystery can also provide a way to enhance and deepen our current educational theory and practice.

Hansen devotes some text in his book to discuss the term "vocation," as it has accreted a number of meanings he wishes to analyze and discuss. He locates this "sense of vocation . . . at the crossroads of public obligation and personal fulfillment."[5] Simple personal fulfillment does not count as vocational as there must be "social value to others." Nor would Hansen count as vocational something that did not yield some personal fulfillment. Vocation is not something that is selfless and ascetic either. When one embarks upon a vocation, one may not be fully convinced or settled, as Hansen further points out.[6] This lack of certainty leads to an opening for the creativity and independence of mind and spirit. This opening is part of successful teaching.

For Hansen, the teachers he studies feel uncomfortable with grand illusions. They are not heroes and do not think of themselves as heroic. Schweitzer was keenly aware of what might be called an occupational hazard of doing good works. This occupational hazard played out publicly for Schweitzer, on a world stage. Most teachers will not have people give up their lives to follow their work as Schweitzer did, and Hansen points out that Schweitzer admonished these would-be disciples to go home. The work Schweitzer undertook at Lambaréné is just too complex and difficult to harbor those with rosy views of selflessly helping the downtrodden. Hansen is sober and forthright on this point, warning that "the language of vocation is all too easily romanticized. Employed uncritically, the concept can trigger images of self-sacrifice and devotion that may be appropriate for the likes of Mother Teresa."[7] Furthermore, the romanticizing of devotion removes the daily acts of teaching from fecund critique where we may learn lessons from such teachers, and also from people like Schweitzer. I first drafted these words in the midst of the 2008 political season, when Barack Obama was criticized for only speaking in "flowery rhetoric," as one of my students stated. What this student and others want is more of what they deem substance that they can engage with and discuss. For this student and others like her, inspiration is simply not enough.

It is difficult to walk the fine line between analysis and inspiration. The work of someone like Schweitzer may inspire one to action, but is frankly beyond what is possible for many. I encountered the same issue in my work with teachers in North Carolina in the 1990s. We established an innovative center for teachers and teaching[8] that was unique in its mission and practice. We were all state employees, so we did not make the level of commitment that Schweitzer did to his work. Yet the dissemination of this center's innovations has remained problematic. Some educators who visited thought they had to replicate what we did, and rued that it was not possible back home. They missed the point that this center, as well as the hospital at Lambaréné, should function as a cultural symbol, an instance of an effort by a group of people at one particular time and place, to bring about change. There are many such opportunities for those who seek to help others, and replication is not such an opportunity. One must find one's own Lambaréné.[9]

In a later chapter, Hansen further explores the confounding dialectic of being called to an active life of teaching. How do you reconcile the passive sense of being called to teach, with the active sense of being attentive?[10] All of the teachers that Hansen discusses are active and attentive to their students. Yet each of them was "called" to teach, some by what he calls the whisper they hear: "try teaching." Schweitzer too explores this dialectic in his memoirs. He was attuned to being called through his sensitivity to suffering, so much so that when hearing the peal of church bells as a boy, he decided then and there to live his life in a certain way. As Hansen puts it when considering why the teachers heard this call to teach, "But what appears natural to a person is often the result of years of activity."[11] We may prepare for a moment that seems transcendent and final with long periods of reflection and analysis, or in the case of being called to teach, by enacting some of the work of a teacher. I recall vividly in my boyhood teaching a younger fellow Boy Scout about knot tying. My scoutmaster listened in on my lesson and said to me, you are a natural teacher. I think of that moment from time to time as I reflect upon the context of the work I have chosen to do.

These incidents that built up in Schweitzer's consciousness are also conditioned by two things that are not usually part of what a typical teacher may encounter: One was the antipathy that Schweitzer felt toward the teaching that he was already doing. This aversion was toward a passive and rote manner of learning that he had been accustomed to in his schooling, and also in the kind of instruction that he was expected to give as a teacher of philosophy and theology. We see repeatedly in the letters between Albert and Hélène the near anguished discussion he had about the expectations that he had for himself and how the dull, rote teaching that he was doing interfered with what he wanted to do and how he wanted to live his life. How different this is from what we see with the teachers that Hansen describes as hearing the call to teach. Schweitzer heard a call to action that led him from his comfortable life of "just being a professor" to forge a new identity, and in that lifework, to become a special kind of teacher within a particular and unusual educational setting, the Lambaréné hospital.

What Hansen says about teaching and "school teaching" is germane here, as he discusses how one forms an identity not in the institution or within the confines of the practice, but in a larger vision.[12] This is what Schweitzer did in Lambaréné, especially when he sought to not have people there who simply wanted to find themselves; they were to seek their own Lambaréné.

> Furthermore, the idea of vocation does not imply the redemptive motive of "saving" others that is associated with some religious and secular practices.
>   Albert Schweitzer used to advise would-be medical helpers who came out to Africa in order to "do something special," as they put it, to go back home unless they understood that the work they could do there was not, as he put it, "something out of the ordinary." Schweitzer would recommend that they turn around unless they had "no thought of heroism" but rather appreciated the sense of a "duty undertaken with sober enthusiasm" (Quoted in Emmet, 1958, p. 254). Schweitzer's counsel implies that along with a desire to engage the world, the sense of vocation presumes a certain mixture of realism and humility, at least in incipient form. Those qualities would seem to make possible a more respectful appraisal of oneself and one's setting.[13]

Lambaréné was not special as simply a hospital in the equatorial jungle, as there were other such hospitals, nor was it unique for a European to dispense missionary medicine. Some of those who sought redemption or direction by coming to Lambaréné were disappointed in the ordinariness of the work there. The ones who stayed learned to have "no thought of heroism" as they faced the repetitive and daunting demands for basic medical care that the Lambaréné hospital struggled to meet.[14]

Reflections for a calling to a life of service

Schweitzer distilled what he thought important from his hard and unheroic work at the hospital in a number of books, articles, and speeches. He also remembered how he started on his path in life by excavating more into his memory. In the final chapter of his narrative about boyhood and growing up, *Memoirs of Childhood and Youth*,[15] Schweitzer considers the things most important in his life that he derived from his childhood. There are six sections to the chapter, each headed with a simple word or phrase. These are the reflections of a middle-aged man upon his youth, derived from the more detailed account of his life in the earlier chapters. There is an almost elegiac tone, recognizing a time that has past, and contemplating on what could have been done otherwise. These six sections form a whole where the pieces interlock and contribute to his mature thinking and to his educational views.

Gratitude

Schweitzer affirms others, especially those he has not recognized fully or appropriately in the past: "When I look back at my youth, I am moved by the thought of how many people I have to thank for what they were to me and what they gave me. At the same time, however, I become depressed when I realize how little I have expressed my gratitude to those people when I was young."[16]

This is a common enough sentiment for any reflective, middle-aged person, especially when one realizes the sacrifices and extra, unheralded work by other people involved in caring for the young. Schweitzer adds a twist of interpretation to this common experience. It is not that youth are necessarily ungrateful, though in fact they may be, but rather that youth do not take the time to express their gratitude. What effect would there be if this were the case? Schweitzer brings up a vivid metaphor, whereby unannounced gratitude is like the plentiful water flowing beneath the surface of the earth, and he believes if only we allowed it to come forth the way a magnificent spring does when the water comes up to the surface, visible to all and nourishing to those who tread upon the abundant stream that lays beneath their feet, would we then realize the power of such gratitude.[17] Gratitude here is fully expressed and reaches its potential. It is an action that is then generative and directed toward others.

Influence

The second recollection is similar to the first on gratitude, in that influence, or the effect one has upon another, is often hidden or overlooked by the young. We do not have enough experience in the world to see our influence, but more than that, influence is an elusive effect, because one can sometimes never know what was one's influence, or to whom or how far it went. For Schweitzer, influence is not instrumental or calculating, but rather fecund and vital, for these people "entered my life and became forces within me."[18] We unconsciously model ourselves after others, and Schweitzer lists the kinds of traits so brought on by influence: "gentleness, kindness, ability to forgive, truthfulness, faithfulness, submission in suffering we owe to people in whom we experience these qualities, whether in an important or unimportant event."[19]

All of these traits are learned *in relation to* another, and are consummately other-regarding. They do not focus on the individual and his or her aggrandizement. As we cannot often see how gratitude works, neither can we be sure of our influence. As teachers, we need to remind ourselves of the ripples we may never see.[20] This makes teaching the young both difficult and rewarding. It is hard for a teacher to see the effect he or she may have, and thus teachers may become discouraged and think they are not producing any satisfying results with their students. Many teachers, however, are lucky to receive word of their influence upon their students, oftentimes years later. I still remember, and want to share here, the lessons of exact reading learned from Edwin Curley, with whom I studied the early modern philosophy of Descartes and Spinoza years ago. He introduced the "reader on my shoulder" to me and asked that I pay attention to what this person might say, usually a whisper asking for clarification and more exact language in the papers I wrote.

If one could be more explicit in gratitude for what one receives, one could then make more explicit the influences one has. Thus, these two traits are related and work together in Schweitzer's scheme of how one matures and acknowledges the path one's education has taken.

Mutual knowledge

For Schweitzer, we are each cloaked in mystery, such that to know another well is ultimately impossible. There are precious few moments when we can get to know another, and these come almost by accident "as if illumined by lightning."[21] This condition of only catching fleeting glimpses of another dictates for Schweitzer that we must not presume too much, and we must live with a deep sense of mutual respect for that mystery. Intruding upon another, whether to give advice or direction is tantamount to disrobing that person:

> Analyzing others—except in order to help mentally confused people—is ignoble. There is not only a bodily, but also a spiritual modesty, which we have to respect. The soul, too, has its cloak, which one should not tear off. None of us must say to another person: because we belong together in such and such a way, I have the right to know all your thoughts. Not even a mother may behave this way toward her child. All demands of this kind are foolish and harmful.[22]

Schweitzer does not limit his view to adults, but applies it to that fundamental educational relationship, mother and child. So, what then should be the way one interacts with another, so as to gain familiarity and knowledge? He thinks that one should "share of your spiritual being as much as you can with those who walk with you on your way and accept as something precious what comes back to you from them."[23] This traveling together on the spiritual journey and respecting another person so as not to intrude, while allowing mutual knowledge to come in if and when it will is the respectful way to be with another person.

Reserve versus Freedom

Schweitzer continues to develop the idea of the respectful soul and how one could show "respect." But too often such "respect" may be reserve, not wanting to engage others due to shyness or cultural norms. Schweitzer's natural shyness was strengthened by his aunt's ideas of reserve being part of good breeding.[24] Yet, he draws a distinction between tact and a reserve that would rob one of engaging others that would lead to mutual benefit and growth. The other may include the stranger in our midst, and from that person we may learn a great deal. As Darrell Fasching argues, the test of ethics is how we treat the stranger.[25] That stranger may be someone we encounter on a street, but also may be the person who deals with and even suffers from disabilities, such as the special education student. What our actions and policies say about how we deal with such "strangeness" may be a way to gauge our ethical maturity. The cultivation of hospitality[26] in the presence of strangers and that to which we are unaccustomed is a goal for us and our schools.

From enthusiasm to "ripeness"

While Schweitzer continues to see our character and soul as essentially mysterious and private, he believes it important to retain a youthful idealism, and not be given over to the confines that adulthood puts upon our outlooks. Though Schweitzer is committed to Enlightenment rationality, he goes beyond a stress upon reason and takes into account the role of emotion in motivation and action. Too often what is mistaken for "maturity" is something that is less than what one believed in one's youth. Schweitzer uses the metaphor of music; maturity has within it discords, described by "the words impoverishment, stunted growth, and blunted feelings."[27] He continues with a stirring passage:

> What is usually considered maturity in a person is really resigned reasonableness. It is acquired by adopting others as models and by abandoning one after another the thoughts and convictions that were dear to us in our youth. We believed in the good; we no longer do so. We were zealous for justice; we are so no longer. We had faith in the power of kindness and peaceableness; we have it no longer. We could be filled with enthusiasm; we can no longer be. In order to navigate more safely through the dangers and storms of life, we lighten our boat. We threw overboard goods that we thought were dispensable; but it was our food and water that we got rid of. Now we travel more lightly, but we are starving.[28]

Schweitzer does not want to merely celebrate youthful idealism and zeal; he wants to harness it to action taken throughout a life's course. He admonishes all who push young people to a conformity borne of fear and uncertainty about the future. Schweitzer is saying we think that the youthful ideals we have are essentially a burden and we mistakenly believe they cloud our vision and our action as we get older. They are supposedly idle ideas, not worthy of the responsibilities and duties of a "mature" person. But are these the ideals that foster and fuel a mature vision? Schweitzer believes emphatically this to be the case. Thus, a demand of maturity is to keep alive these ideals, to seek ways to act according to them, and to not become disillusioned.

Idealism

This section is a continuation, and culmination, of the discussion. One should not become too ripe or used up, but maintain one's youthful enthusiasm. Schweitzer says that youth are almost naturally passionate for the "ideas that fill them with enthusiasm throughout their lives."[29] Many give up these views in the face of a reality closing in on them. The Wordsworthian "shades of the prison house begin to close upon the growing Boy" but like the light that saves the boy, so do the ideals we hold as children nourish us later. As Schweitzer remarks, "When ideals collide with reality, they are usually crushed by facts. That, however, does not mean that ideals have to capitulate before facts to begin with. It only means that our ideals are not strong enough. They are not strong enough because they are not sufficiently pure, firm, and stable within us."[30]

Weak ideals for Schweitzer are nothing more than mere ideas. For these ideas to become what he considers ideals, they must be acted upon. His poetic version of this activity, using water, ice, and gas[31] does not elaborate in any detail how this might happen. We are left with an equally incomplete assertion about ideas and ideals in this statement: "The power becomes effective only when they are thought by a noble human being."[32] How does this "taking up" become accomplished? What kinds of circumstances or environments—schooling, contact with others—best encourage such development? We get no answers here to these questions. Instead, Schweitzer simply states:

> So the knowledge about life which we grown-ups must impart to the young is not: "Reality will surely do away with your ideals" but rather: "Grow into your ideals so life cannot take them away from you." If people were to become what they are at age fourteen, how very different the world would be![33]

For Schweitzer, ultimately, these ideals become incarnated in the person who lives by kindness and example. And this goal, to "think and live thoughts of love, truth, peaceableness and gentleness with sufficient purity of heart and steadfastness"[34] will eventually issue forth into a new world, where all are regarded as such. How this aim can be realized is the task of the kind of education that draws its support from Schweitzer, but with a more defined and practical realization of his poetic/philosophical thoughts I shall outline later.

5

Reverence for Life

In his twenties, Schweitzer grew frustrated with the pessimism of many of his university friends and colleagues, thinking them spectators dissecting the past and not living in the present and into the future. He turned from theology and philosophy to something more directly practical, tropical medicine, and a life in Africa. For Schweitzer, civilization now had become external and lifeless, especially as manifest in the science and technology of his day, where a hollow sense of progress was not matched by an ethical maturation, but by a naïve belief in the power of reason to solve all problems. He briefly sketches his philosophy of civilization in his autobiography[1] while charting this course of events more fully in *Civilization and Ethics*.[2] Schweitzer characterized reason as having a magnificent run of it, but that in the great nineteenth-century German philosophers (Fichte, Schelling, and Hegel), the grand system of reason became exhausted by relying merely upon itself: "Reason alone cannot provide an interpretation of the world that assigns a course of ethical action for man."[3] Though he admired the primacy of reason that was a major legacy of the Enlightenment, Schweitzer saw that reason by itself could not provide cultural and ethical vitality.

Beyond the Inheritance of the Past

Though Schweitzer considered writing a book called *Wir Epigonen* (*We Inheritors of the Past*)[4] he determined that this was not a constructive way out of this malaise. True to his intellectual outlook and character, he wanted to find a bedrock principle or principles upon which to ground his life. Schweitzer was not, as Jackson Lee Ice has pointed out,[5] a systematic ethicist. Criticisms by others that he did not provide a systemic ethical theory are valid, but importantly, they miss the point of his work. Schweitzer was more concerned with finding a generative wellspring that could animate his life and actions as well as that of others.[6]

Schweitzer valued independence of thought and wanted others to think for themselves, but he realized that such a task could be thwarted by the situation in which one finds oneself:

> The spirit of the age never lets him find himself. Over and over again, convictions are forced upon him just as he is exposed, in big cities, to glaring neon signs of companies that are rich enough to install them and enjoin him at every step to give preference to one or another shoe polish or soup mix.[7]

What this spirit does is force people into a kind of herd mentality, so that they are not thinking for themselves but want others to do this for them. It is a lack of confidence, for "in spite of his great technological achievements and material possession, he is an altogether stunted being, because he makes no use of his capacity for thinking."[8]

It is by activity, and engagement with others, that such an affirmation toward positive action is accomplished. Schweitzer struggles along to try to ground his life in his ideals and do something constructive and not be merely part of the end-of-century pessimism, where he "felt like someone who has to replace a rotten boat that is no longer seaworthy with a new and better one, but does not know how to proceed."[9] He sought a core principle to affirm civilization and to make it whole from the inside out, not merely from the outside in terms of science, progress, and power.

In 1913, he took a journey up the Ogooué River from Lambaréné:

> Lost in thought I sat on the deck of the barge, struggling to find the elementary and universal concept of the ethical that I had not discovered in any philosophy. I covered sheet after sheet with disconnected sentences merely to concentrate on the problem. Two days passed. Late on the third day, at the very moment when, at sunset, we were making our way through a herd of hippopotamuses, there flashed upon my mind, unforeseen and unsought, the phrase "reverence for life." The iron door had yielded. The path in the thicket had become visible. Now I had found my way to the principle in which affirmation of the world and ethics are joined together![10]

He finally came to that foundation upon which he could base his life's work, something toward which he had been striving since, at least, his scholarship on Kant and Jesus as a young man. The metaphors used by Schweitzer indicate just how urgent this task was for his soul. A boat that one needs to navigate through life had become "rotten" and the way out toward a fresh and seaworthy boat was through an "iron door." Schweitzer called this principle Reverence for Life and this simple utterance, come upon with clarity and force in what initially appear to be unlikely circumstances, anchored his entire thought henceforth.[11]

Schweitzer achieved this insight, like Descartes did with his *cogito*, by a reverie where he withdrew and focused upon what was elemental and foundational. This Cartesian move had a different emphasis however. Descartes wanted to find what was indubitable, and upon it built his rationalism. Unlike Descartes' *cogito*, however, Schweitzer's Reverence for Life moves one outward to a connection with a larger whole that is Nature and other living beings. There is recognition that existence is "unfathomably mysterious" and reciprocity with other living things, in granting the same kind of feeling toward oneself that you feel toward the other. This is what Schweitzer means when he says that "(man) experiences that other life *in* his own,"[12] and furthermore Reverence for Life extends to Nature and that which gives for all that lives this same reverence.

What Schweitzer calls the "ethical acceptance of the world"[13] means that the world itself is accepted or affirmed and our part within it is interdependent. We recognize this interdependence and affirm our need to do what is the Good to keep Nature robust and life-giving. We need to do what is the Good not only to improve social conditions for humans, but to recognize and realize our place within Nature.

The Idea of Reverence

What can we say to more fully understand this core principle of Schweitzer? To begin to get at this question, it is useful to discuss the idea of reverence historically and philosophically, with the groundwork being a definition of the term. Reverence arises from a profound comprehension of human limitation, frailty, and finitude, prompting awe and wonder at the incomprehensible. It chastens us to live between extremes of excessive egotism and excessive modesty. In education, as in religion and science these days, most assume empirical knowledge is supreme and the aesthetic and even ethical domains are secondary to experienced knowledge. Reverence enables us to create a moral narrative etched by the character of our conduct.

The classicist Paul Woodruff gives a capsule definition of reverence that suits our purposes: Reverence is "the capacity for a range of feelings and emotions that are linked. It is a sense that there is something larger than a human being, accompanied by capacities for awe, respect, and shame; it is often expressed in, and reinforced by, ceremony."[14] A caveat here is appropriate: Reverence does not mean mute and prim solemnity, for that is a caricature of this virtue. One can express reverence with joy and spontaneity. Ceremonies of reverence invoke feelings of shared veneration and wonder at the kind of higher meanings and values that connect individuals together in a community, such as truth, learning, and justice, along with the educational institutions and practices that transmit them across generations. Virtues are learned by participating in shared social practices. Such rituals and ceremonies help cultivate the virtue of reverence.

Reverence and virtue

Woodruff argues that reverence is a "cardinal virtue,"[15] by which he means that, like courage, justice, or temperance, we can find forms of it in many, though perhaps not all, cultures. Virtue ethics is concerned with the quality and content of our character. The organizing question of modern ethics has tended to be, "What are we morally obligated to do?" Answers to this question yield "duty" ethics, where the organizing question is, "How may what I do be universally applied?," or "consequentialist" ethics, where one asks, "How many will benefit by this action?" The organizing question of ancient ethics was usually, "What kind of person is it best to be?" and answers to this question yield virtue ethics. There has been a renaissance in virtue ethics over the last few decades.

Virtue ethics concerns itself with attitudes, values, habits of action, imagination, emotions, interests, perceptions, and desires that serve as motives for individual action. Virtue emphasizes three things, captured by these terms from ancient Greek: *Arête, phronesis,* and *eudaimonia. Arête* refers to excellence or virtue; moral virtues include honesty, generosity, care, compassion, toleration, preservation of well-being, and many other traits of character. In a virtuous person, these traits blend and balance each other in ways that vary according to the context of action. Virtue ethics also emphasizes *phronesis,* or practical wisdom. Such practical wisdom depends on worldly experience. *Phronesis* involves moral perception—that is, sensitivity to the concrete particulars of a situation as well as moral imagination that grasps the best possibilities within the given situation. The goal is to live a fulfilled and happy life (*eudaimonia*) of meaning and value to one's self and community. Virtue ethics is often criticized for being culturally relative, excessively situational, without systematic justification, and unable to provide the kind of action guidance associated with rules and regulations. However, its emphasis on qualities of character, embodied disposition, practical wisdom, and happiness are valuable and too often overlooked.

Reverence is often more a matter of emotional and imaginative perception than cognition, although that too is important. Reverence involves awe, wonder, and imagination, regarding something or someone, though the object of reverence may vary. Woodruff observes that "the principal object of reverence is something that reminds us of human limitation."[16] Here, I am primarily concerned with reverence for life, justice, love, truth, possibility, ideals, and human potential; however, that simply represents interests for this discussion related to education and Schweitzer. Reverence for God, Nature, death,[17] and much more are perfectly appropriate for other discussions and situations.

Feelings of respect arise from reverence as naturally as awe, wonder, and admiration. When the members of a community share reverence for something greater than any of the individuals who constitute the community, then the individual community members should show a degree of respect for every other member. For instance, we all share human life; we are all mortal, we all know love, joy, and sorrow, and we all hope and dream. Reverence for the human condition can unite us across vast differences of culture and religion. It may well be the supreme virtue of the multicultural classroom. Here teachers and students can offer, appreciate, and analyze different viewpoints, cultural biases, and pre-sumptions about what matters in life in the context of hearing them out and seeing them not only as nuanced and heartfelt, but also as unexamined and rote.

The experience we have as human beings is that we all feel pain, suffer, grieve, and die. We too may also all know peace, joy, and enduring life through our children. Reverence for Life is twofold for Schweitzer: We express care and compassion for suffering, bearing witness to what other humans endure, as we are part of that suffering, while seeking and cele-brating joy and peace. A teacher's reverence for life in the classroom can compassionately ameliorate suffering while seeking to bring about and celebrate joy.

Mutual respect in devotion to a shared ideal may bind people together even when it is obvious that some should be held in much higher esteem than others because of their superior wisdom, moral character, or ability. All are equally humbled before the might of the mystery. Even criminals or classroom mischief-makers deserve a modicum of respect when it comes time to distribute justice. That is why we should moderate the severity of our judgment when the transgressor is contrite. Just law transcends all our actions. In schools, classroom discipline should be reverent; it should never be an ego struggle between teacher and student. Teachers must show special respect in helping someone who is ignorant and only requires care and attention in learning to come to a better understanding. Reverent teachers will acknowledge their own limitations.

Reverence is a virtue and thus an embodied habit of action that guides appropriate feelings to their proper objects. Like any other habit, practice helps make accustomed, if not quite perfect. Reverent practice involves rituals and ceremonies that properly orient the practitioner toward right action in accordance with the object of reverence (e.g., idea, ideal, and so on). Social rituals orient the entire community in showing respect for the object of reverence and for each other. Irreverence means showing a lack of respect for something that or someone who is generally taken seriously by others.

Reverence is a virtue, but sometimes, so too is irreverence. If, upon careful reflection, something is not deserving of reverence, we should not act reverently toward it. Sometimes, irreverence is the proper attitude; indeed, it is what true reverence demands. Reflective inquiry should lead to irreverence when something is an imposter, when something claims it is worthy of reverence when in fact it is not. On the other hand, in our times, there seems to be a tendency to mock even the highest and best. On such occasions, irreverence is the greatest folly. It destroys individuals and communities by corrupting virtuous action. We fail to feel shame when we should, our rituals become empty, and we do not respect others with whom we share values. When irreverence overcomes everything of worth, we have entered an era of nihilism that destroys all values human or transcendent and all of life's existential meaning. We may be just "amusing ourselves to death"[18] with the chatter of popular media and deceiving ourselves into thinking that we are creating meaning.

Virtues such as reverence belong to communities as moral customs just as they belong to individuals as habits of good conduct. Although I am interested in the community of practice designated by the occupation of teaching, especially the classroom community, I am also concerned with the school and the larger community. Virtues are oriented toward what are considered the ideals, goods, and values of a practice, whether it be firefighting, finance, or teaching. Reverent classrooms cultivate appropriate awe, wonder, admiration, respect, and shame, often by proper ritual, in pursuit of shared ideals of human flourishing.

Reverence for Life

Reverence for Life is a special term for Schweitzer and perhaps his most famous utterance. He uses it for the basis of a universal concept of ethics. He believed that such an ethics, as circumscribed by this term, would reconcile the drives of altruism and egoism by requiring a respect for the lives of all other beings, and by demanding the highest development of an individual's moral resources. The original German gives us more meaning, however. "*Ehrfurcht vor dem Leben*" is difficult to translate to English. The German *ehrfurcht* is akin to the English *awe*, namely that which we feel atop mountain, at a storm at sea, or on watching a tornado bearing down upon a Midwestern cornfield. For Schweitzer, of course, the immediate context was the African jungle, in its overwhelming power and mystery, but also fellow human beings who are just as fundamentally unknown.

In translating Schweitzer's grounding principle of "*Ehrfurcht vor dem Leben*," we encounter the immense, almost incomprehensive quality of the very idea of reverence. Respect in English or French falls short of capturing the full meaning. Yet, even the English word "reverence" does not amply or aptly translate the German word "*Ehrfurcht*," which connotes awe and majesty (*Ehre*: honor; "*Furcht*": fear).[19] Furthermore, the German word connotes a sense of being humble in the face of all living things *and* a sense of responsibility to them.[20] The tragic sense of *Furcht* or fear also underlies this sensibility, which is concealed by the English translation "Reverence for Life."[21] *Ehrfurcht* is a product of a particular kind of thought. It is not step-by-step rational, linear, thinking, but rather the dwelling of thought, a meditative consideration, a taking in, that is conveyed by the German verb *Denken*. This kind of thinking (*Denken*) is inextricably tied to both building (*Bauen*) and dwelling (*Wohnen*) for Martin Heidegger:

> Building and thinking are, each in its own way, inescapable for dwelling. The two, however, are also insufficient for dwelling so long as each busies itself with its own affairs in separation instead of listening to one another. They are able to listen if both—building and thinking—belong to dwelling, if they remain within their limits and realize that the one as much as the other comes from the workshop of long experience and incessant practice.[22]

Thus, it is a meditative and intentional practice by which this kind of thinking develops and comes alive, and what Schweitzer experienced that day on the river.

Schweitzer's Reverence for Life has been criticized as vague and impractical, or simply a motto. Some critics state that Schweitzer had not developed a strict ethical system using the dictum as a foundation. In this book, I am interested in how Schweitzer's formulation can be used to ground moral thinking in our schools, where I see that the lack of such a foundation enables different and competing ethical claims to not be fully examined. I see Reverence for Life as more a way of being in the world, and an insight into the nature of life itself. It was not Schweitzer's achievement to create a new moral code, but in searching for a way to bind us all together. Yet there are ways that we may use Reverence for Life in the schools that take advantage of some different meanings. Jackson Lee Ice has striven to give an analysis of the term to show how it may be understood if one wants to counter the critique that it is a vague and imprecise motto.

Ice first says that Reverence for Life can be interpreted as having a biological or instinctive function that we respect the will to live. While this is certainly a minor meaning of the term, I don't see this as being particularly compelling in a school setting, other than as an admonition as part of an overall educational aim. A second formulation would be one of self-affirmation, in the case of my own life: "Thus Reverence for Life characterizes the discovery of what it means to respect myself and to realize my own life-giving potentialities. A lack of respect for ourselves makes us our own worst enemies."[23] Though I could see some application of this to schoolchildren, the best application of this formulation would be for teachers. Teachers are notorious for putting others before themselves, and giving to others before they take into account their own needs.

Teachers, particularly in U.S. public schools, spend much of their time in mental and physical "egg crates"[24] where they are isolated from others who might provide mental and emotional support, as well as from just being able to share ideas and have adult conversations. Thus teachers, one to a room as one egg is to its own compartment in a crate-like container, are limited in the amount of their growth. They also expect of themselves that they will give to others first, before their own needs have been taken care of. Of course, this does not apply to all teachers, as there are saints and knaves in teaching as much as in other professions or jobs, but for the most part, in my experience of working with schoolteachers in several places in the United States, this is their mindset.

This blends well into the third of Ice's ideas on Reverence for Life. The dictum can be interpreted as being about a proclivity toward love and concern. Ice believes we need to acknowledge the joining of the ego and the other, as the two elements of our psyche that need to be brought together. Much of what education is all about today in industrialized nations is an education for instrumentality, to gain better jobs, to perform tasks better, to gain technical and useful knowledge to use in the workplace, to get ahead.

This formulation of a meaning of Reverence for Life focuses not only on an inner development, that is, an acknowledgement of the ego and its limitations, but to see that the ego itself needs to be nested in a development of that which is outer, namely the other, or the social context. It is close to what the philosopher John Dewey saw as important as not just a joining of the two, inner and outer, ego and other, individual and society, but recognition of the basic union of the two. The lone individual does not make sense ontologically apart from a social context. They are together originally, and have been separated only by thinkers who got it wrong according to Dewey and others. Reverence for Life acknowledges this union.

Reverence for Life and Natural Piety

Schweitzer's Reverence for Life can be connected to a number of thinkers as discussed in the chapter on philosophical and religious heritage and more explicitly to Goethe's threefold reverence in *Wilhelm Meister's Lehrjahre.* Schweitzer has not been compared to John Dewey, yet there are parallels in their thought and practice. Dewey was 16 years Schweitzer's senior, and there is little evidence that they dealt with each other's thought.[25] Dewey's roots in a religiously informed worldview are well documented[26] if not emphasized in the current revival of his work. His "natural piety" developed from Wordsworth sees human beings as part of Nature, not separate from it. The following passage from Dewey's *A Common Faith* illustrates this view:

> Our successes are dependent upon the cooperation of nature. The sense of the dignity of human nature is as religious as is the sense of awe and reverence when it rests upon a sense of human nature as a cooperating part of a larger whole. Natural piety is not of necessity either a fatalistic acquiescence in natural happenings or a romantic idealization of the world. It may rest upon a just sense of nature as the whole of which we are parts, while it also recognizes that we are parts that are marked by intelligence and purpose, having the capacity to strive by their aid to bring conditions into greater consonance with what is humanly desirable. Such piety is an inherent constituent of a just perspective in life.[27]

Note here that Dewey links a sense of reverence with seeing human nature in a cooperative and symbiotic relationship with "a larger whole." That is, we recognize that we are nested in Nature, not only joined to it, but constitutive of it in our reciprocal relations. Toward these relations, we should have a sense of awe and reverence that for Dewey is "religious." He rests this claim upon his distinction between religion and the religious, much in the same way that Schweitzer does between his Christian faith and what he later termed "ethical mysticism." Dewey deems religion to be something outside the ken of human affairs, there to provide solace and comfort, whereas the religious is part of what we may encounter daily, and serves to bond us to Nature.

Schweitzer clearly saw the good for humans as being part of a larger natural and social fabric, and hearkens back to Amos, Isaiah, Zarathustra, and Confucius as thinkers who sought to affirm the good in others and to improve social conditions. Though Schweitzer was a devoted Christian, he thought traditional, orthodox Christianity had lost its bearings and "ceased to be a creative force in civilization, as we have ample opportunity to see in our own times."[28]

One of the major threats to an inspired and fecund culture was what Schweitzer called the "machine age"[29] that masked what he believed was essential for humans to live in peace and ethical consideration. Schweitzer saw that this age of machines gave us material progress but caused spiritual loss. The way out is to affirm a reverence for life and to live in its simplicity.

Projects of Love and Practical Reverence

In summing up his book on Schweitzer, Mike W. Martin endeavors to show that Reverence for Life has relevance in today's world:

> Reverence for life yokes together all reasonable values as contributing to development of life. In doing so, it especially highlights the ideals of authenticity, compassion, gratitude, justice and peace. It invites us to build on natural desires for self-development and empathy, and to continually widen the circle of our moral concern as part of being at home in the universe. And it inspires us to undertake projects of love through which we experience unity with life. Ethics begins from within, unfolds in self-realization, and finds completion in an ever-widening community of love.[30]

Martin's words are evocative and vivid yet vague. What does "yokes together all reasonable values" and "highlights the ideals" mean in the first two sentences? We yoke things together, gather them; Reverence for Life is a cardinal virtue and thus gathers together values under itself. But not only do cardinal virtues span and gather other virtues as a driver does the reins of his team of horses, they are generative, as Martin states succinctly here. These virtues contribute to "development of life" but do so with added power, so to speak, of the generative cardinal virtue. Martin's use of the verb "highlights" in the second sentence masks this generative power of the cardinal virtue, as this usage here connotes a more passive role of notification to the cardinal virtue of reverence in moral development. Reverence for life does much more than point out these ideals, and fortunately Martin recovers this vitality in the following sentences. The power of Schweitzer's maxim lies in inspiration rather than systematic moral reasoning, and elsewhere he states that Reverence for Life is a "unified, motivating, optimistic ethics of ideals as guides for conduct." [31]

Martin sees Reverence for Life inspiring "projects of love." Love is not a rule or a maxim to be pronounced and followed. Desire as fellow feeling and as Eros seeks the good. Such virtues we see every day in the actions of those who show compassion for animals, nurture children, build lives together, and also, importantly, develop an inner sense of morality. The productive and inspiring power of Schweitzer's insight is there in those who instruct and guide the young in our schools. The idea of practical reverence is developed in educational settings from the home, to Rousseau's Émile guided back through self-exploration in Nature to the "the hands of the author of Things," [32] to the teacher working alongside a student, learning together in classrooms in today's schools. In the next section, I turn to Schweitzer's educational legacy—his idea of practical reverence in teaching and learning.

Part II

Schweitzer and Education

6

Practical Reverence and Education

Schweitzer's wife and life partner, Hélène Bresslau, worked with him to uncover, strengthen, encourage, and shape his ideals. Schweitzer's resolve and determination to go to Africa took hold during his growing relationship with Hélène. Then, during his early years in Africa, while struggling to establish his hospital in Lambaréné, he found the bedrock ethical principle he had been seeking in Reverence for Life.

As Schweitzer understood it, Reverence for Life calls for a display of concern and attention for all of life no matter the species or how a particular living thing affects human beings. Here is where he parted from the anthropocentricism of Goethe and drew instead upon the Jainist nonviolence and noninjury doctrine of ahimsā. Schweitzer is, of course, well known for the lengths and troubles he went to in order to preserve living organisms at Lambaréné. He was portrayed in popular media as kindly but misguided in his insistence upon stepping around insects and such. Such anecdotal and journalistic accounts of his core principle mask its power and seriousness, but these accounts also hamper seeing this principle as something that could be practical in education.

The power of the dictum of Reverence for Life can be used to help enact a set of different measures and attitudes toward Nature and Others in our schools. For example, research into the way children learn about nurturing behavior has shown that boys, in particular, can be encouraged to be caring and generous human beings by tending to companion animals at an early age.[1] Yet by far the most important meaning of Reverence for Life in an educational context is its prescriptive function, declaring what we ought to do. Here it can be enacted within the process of curricular planning as a guiding maxim to judge how the teaching and learning environment will be constructed. Reverence for Life then becomes an ideal that is practical within educational theory and practice, what I term "practical reverence."

Practical Reverence

I use this term to resonate with Schweitzer's idea of practical eschatology, where he looks at human society from a vantage point of reflection while still acting in the world by relieving suffering and encouraging service to others. As Ara Paul Barsam notes, Schweitzer's practical eschatology draws its strength from the "continued relevance of Jesus" that "rests—among other ways—in the espousal of eschatological hope that affords a distance from present institutions."[2] But for Schweitzer there is also the connection to the present, and the infusion of future eschatological hope with present conditions:

> The Messianic consciousness of the uniquely great Man of Nazareth sets up a struggle between the *present* and the *beyond*, and introduces that resolute absorption of the beyond by the present . . . of which we are conscious in ourselves as the essence of religious progress and experience—a process of which the end is not yet in sight.[3]

Certainly the practice of practical reverence in our schools does not demand a Messianic consciousness. However, Schweitzer's point about the conflict and struggle between the present and the beyond or future is germane. The future may bring redemption and eschatological resolution for the religious Christian, but our aim is more modest and circumscribed, if not at least as powerful. To wit, if we argue that reverence, and particularly Reverence for Life, is central to the kind of teaching and leadership needed in today's education, we must acknowledge first the obvious, that reverence is in retreat, not only in the schools, where it is hardly present, but in society in general, by which I mean that society I know best, in the twenty-first century United States of America. If we are to make reverence again a part of human life in our communities then a good place to practice this is in our schools. Can reverence be made practical for teachers, principals, and superintendents given the demands and expectations placed on them? Isn't it a bit odd to talk about "practical reverence?"

The American educator Horace Mann used a metaphor he thought all could understand when he sought support for the common school in the nineteenth century: Children are like wax, not iron, and can be molded. Mann meant that it is not impossible to teach older people and to change their ways, but like iron, they can be obdurate and resistant. Children are far less so, and thus to form a lifetime of good habit and character, we should focus on teaching the young. In addition, there is a burden in teaching the young, because the habits and teachings they learn will eventually become more resistant to change, and perhaps even calcified into rigid attitudes and outlooks. We have the opportunity to get it right, or at least try to do so, with the young. If we want to have a reverent American society that is equipped to overcome the darkness of our imperial moment, it is perhaps best to emphasize the work that remains for our youngest citizens to recover, mold, and sustain the forgotten virtue of reverence. The self thus enacted is reverential in that it acknowledges limitations and dependencies.[4] Many of the virtues aside from Puritanical hard work and delayed gratification seem superfluous when education is viewed instrumentally, as a linear means to a fixed and predetermined end. Educational attainment is thus measured and subject to standards and accountability practices such as the American educational mandate of the No Child Left Behind Act.[5]

Reverent Teachers

If we are to treat reverence practically in our schools, we should begin to identify those traits of reverent teachers. Such traits include showing awe and wonder before the subject matter they teach. These teachers also have deep respect for their students while seeking to deserve their respect. Reverent teachers show strong leadership and include others in their deliberations. They also understand the importance of ritual and ceremony in establishing classroom and school community. I know where I got these ideas, and perhaps this is the same for you: Observing teachers and reflecting on my own teaching, I value the people I work with and the students I teach. I see that there is so much I do not know. Similarly, I don't fully know my colleagues or my students, and one cannot know anyone fully, as Schweitzer reminds us. Thus, I am humble before the subject matter at hand, even if it is an area where I have had some education. It is harder to be humble before others, particularly if I find the person's behavior objectionable or even reprehensible, so I need to remind myself to keep trying to understand the other person. These are reverent traits. Likewise, I realize that social support and the bonds of community are critical for good educational practice. I believe what builds these bonds are practices such as ritual and ceremony, and attitudes replete with awe and wonder.

Awe and wonder

Reverent teachers know that the inheritance of culture and knowledge they receive and bestow is not solely of their making. They have a sense for the humanity, departed, present, and yet to be born in the subject matter taught and the values actualized. They know we live by the grace of the knowledge and wisdom realized by those who have gone before. Reverent teachers exemplify the good of their practice. These teachers are never arrogant or presumptuous toward their students, for they know that as their students stand to the teacher's superior knowledge so too do they as teachers stand toward the superior wisdom of both the subject matter they teach and of those who preceded them. They are humbled by their sense of limitation, but emboldened to teach and learn actively and continuously.

Knowledge

Reverent teachers listen carefully to what the subject matter has to say to them, but they also listen carefully to what their students say to them as well. Teachers must not only know their subject matter, but also their students. To do this successfully, they must accept the risk and vulnerability of openness to what their students suggest, and what they might not know themselves as teachers. That means good teachers must have the moral perception and imagination to connect to students and the intellectual command of subject matter to readily reconfigure it. Both require a kind of learning unique to the practice of teaching. Teaching is not just about the transmission of knowledge or even its expansion. Its calling is higher than that, for teaching seeks wisdom beyond knowledge alone by applying knowledge to life, especially the life of students and the larger community, and thereby to express life itself. Reverent listening to both students and subject matter greatly aids this kind of teaching and learning.

Modeling

Teachers are leaders, and one of the most important things leaders do is provide fine examples of what it is they practice. John Dewey observes that in communicating an experience to someone "you will find your own attitude toward your experience changing."[6] Genuine communication always respects the other with whom you are communicating. This is especially so in teaching where what is taught must be reconfigured to connect to the cognitive, emotional, and material conditions of the student. One cannot connect and model until they have listened and learned about what others need, desire, and dream. Part of the Deweyan ideal of a participatory democratic classroom is that everyone learns together, which does not presuppose they are learning the same thing though they are studying the same subject matter. At the same time, they are also studying each other.

Respect

Reverent teaching involves respect. Woodruff asserts: "Respect is given, not earned."[7] His reversal of the usual form of this bromide is important. We may respect others, including our students solely based on our common humanity. There is also the sharing of common practices and ideals; at the very least, there are the ideas and values of the subject matter that teachers and students must more or less master. Finally, teaching is a caring profession where teachers seek to share their values of self-transcending care, concern, and compassion. This sharing involves listening, as respect should be reciprocal; such mutual respect arises readily out of shared commitments.

Promoting mutual respect in the presence of higher values shared by all provides a better climate for classroom discipline. For example, everyone shares similar needs for personal recognition and fair play. Mutual respect for these values readily leads to mutual respect for others in the everyday give-and-take of classroom interaction. Obedience is better when the ultimate authority lies beyond everyone, teacher, student, and principal alike, and all agree to submit to it because they feel it is legitimate.

Transcendence

Reverence attends to the call of transcendent value that binds us all, ranging from the voice of the whining, deceitful child who appeals to justice when all they want is his or her selfish advantage to the plaintive cry of those who suffer the beatings, emotional and otherwise, of bullies. Often we cannot name what we hear, but we can still feel it. Indeed, good teaching practice can succeed without consciously knowing "that" something is thus and so. Good practice is secured by simply knowing "how" to do something the right way at the right time even if one cannot give the right reason.[8] Reverent listening depends on the ability to literally embody in one's habits of conduct these appropriate practices. Katherine Schultz speaks of teachers learning to "pay attention to the talk in classrooms, making sense of the meanings of students' utterances and through this talk tracking participation and understanding."[9] However, Schultz is particularly interested in learning to listen to silences. While her point is to help teachers know "that" they should attend not only to overt utterances and to silence, many fine teachers already know "how" to do it, although they could not state any of the right reasons Schultz provides. It would be unsurprising if Schultz herself did not first engage in good listening practice long before she figured out how to render it explicit.

Limits

Reverent teaching recognizes that any individual is limited in judgment. Wise teachers of first graders realize that while they know much more than their students, they cannot make judgments that build a good learning community by themselves. They must listen to their very young students and sense what are the incipient good habits of character and community that are being formed. A good classroom environment involves shared deliberation about the good, the right, and the customs of conduct all must embody. Good deliberation must be continuous and ongoing if it is to be self-correcting. Teachers thus need to constantly revisit, and sometimes revise, rules about toy sharing, proper lunchroom decorum, and what constitutes fair play. Democratic deliberation in schools is not about voting whether or not to learn today, rather, it is about the values and practices of good learning, and how each individual fits into the community.

Such deliberation allows teachers to listen to the concerns of the students so that they may make better decisions, but it also reminds them they must listen to the higher meanings and values of teaching, of learning, of subject matter, and of humanity that bind them as much as it does their students. It also protects the teacher from hubris, overconfidence, arrogance, and improper use of power and control. Reverent listening in teaching accepts the risk and vulnerability of opening oneself to the other; it accepts criticism and remains creatively responsive. Beyond all other considerations, reverent teaching understands the need to listen and respect students, parents, custodial staff, secretaries, and principals. Reverent teachers value the merit of ideas, rather than the supposed status of the source. Thus, a good, or bad, idea can come from a colleague as well as a student, a superintendent as well as a custodian.

Ritual and Ceremony

A ritual is a familiar and repeated action that an individual or group performs to give structure to their lives. Objects or actions are accorded meaning. In the example discussed later, a teacher reads to students from a particular chair at a certain time. Ceremonies are composed of rituals that mark particularly meaningful occasions, such as a school commencement or the inauguration of a new school leader. Ritual and ceremony provide the space for us to hear and enable reverential listening.[10] These tangible representations of reverence expressed in ritual and ceremony are largely absent or perverted in many school cultures. The pep rally described in H. G. Bissinger's *Friday Night Lights*[11] exhibits no vital connection of athletics to many of the central purposes of school such as academic achievement and growth. Rather, the football players and cheerleaders aggrandize and display themselves for the entertainment and supposed adulation of their classmates, and indeed, the entire community.

Reverent teaching honors shared ceremony and ritual. Ritual helps organize and structure the classroom community around common beliefs, values, and the virtues of classroom practice. A fourth grade teacher gathers students around her as she sits in a large rocking chair reading aloud, reviewing and revising class rules, or making announcements. It is part of the class's daily ritual and demands, and receives respect and attention. The most remarkable quality of this ritual, however, is that students also sit in the chair when they read stories, poems, or such of their own composition, when they have something to show or tell, or when they want to express a concern that involves classroom conduct. This chair is reserved for occasions of some consequence that involve the interests of all members of the community.[12] Ceremony too, such as a school or college commencement, and the attendant ritual of switching a cap tassel to the left, signal to the participants their incipient place in the larger community and its greater good.

In a good community, one's place is not fixed but dynamic and alters as the needs of the community may require. The ritual of the rocking chair elevates whoever sits in it by making their thoughts, feeling, and actions a matter of shared concern. The teacher is firmly in charge, but she created a ceremony that respected everyone and where each child participated. The rocking-chair ritual received respect even amid disagreements because it involved activities valued and respected by all. Performing the rituals of reverent teaching invokes feelings of belonging to a greater unity in spite of differences.

Silence and Humility

Though reverent listening in teaching can be active and engaged, it may be more powerfully enacted when listening for and to silence. Katherine Schultz[13] discusses the topic of listening to silence in classrooms in ways that are often reverential. She discusses respect for students and urges us, following Dewey, Freire, and other progressive and critical educators, to consider that teachers should create openings and opportunities in their talk that accommodate students who might otherwise maintain a subjugated silence. Such open-endedness allows teachers to explore subject matter with students, or at least not inhibit the student's exploration. It even allows teachers to humbly admit that they do not know the answer to a good question, or, perhaps, that no one knows given the current state of the subject matter.

Schultz also listens for and recognizes instances that might be called silence without reverence. She provides several sad examples of bullying and arrogance, mostly by teachers. Below, Woodruff describes a kind of student not mentioned by Schultz in her paper, but one that we are sure she knows all too well. It is a particular kind of arrogant student who silences other students, and sometimes teachers:

> The worst violator and the one that is most difficult for teachers to handle is the loud student. Confident in his own brilliance, hugely vocal, and often male, the dominant student does not seem to hear what another student, or even the teacher, has to say in discussion, so intent is he on presenting his own views. He speaks as if he has nothing to learn from others . . . Instead, he takes the class as ground on which he can exercise his power to control a conversation. Other students fall into resentful silence.[14]

Often teachers aid and abet such lack of reverence. The tragedy, like that of *King Lear*, arises from a failure to listen carefully and respect the speech as well as the unnatural silence of subordinates. We often find calamity, sadness, and lack of reverence in the same place. Likewise good fortune, joy, and reverence often reside together.

Reverence between Teachers and Students

I spent part of a year observing and interacting with a teacher and her students in a classroom full of animals. The school is located on the edge of a small university city in Indiana, where children of professors, other white-collar workers, farmers, and laborers are all mixed together.

This classroom buzzed with activity as the children cared for the pet gerbils, snakes, hamsters, and guinea pigs. These pets were not simply there as diversions from the teaching and learning activities of a structured, state-mandated curriculum. Rather, the teacher involved the students in caring for the animals. Students needed to learn that animals require constant and systematic care and attention. Some students knew more about animal care than others, particularly those children raised on farms or in homes with domestic animals or pets. But what allowed reverence for the mystery of life to erupt in the classroom was unexpected. "She had babies last night," the children shrieked as they noticed the mother guinea pig nursing her young one morning. The children took care of these babies, and even learned how they could sell them and use those funds to purchase food and litter for the mother. Later, when one of the other animals, a hamster, died, the class held a funeral, complete with a ceremony and short testimonials.

They learned some lessons in biology and economics in caring for the pets, but they also enacted reverence for the mystery of birth and death. Many of these children had no firsthand experience in seeing another creature give birth or die. But their reactions to these life-changing events were entirely appropriate: spontaneous joy at birth, and respectful silence at death. How did these children know what to do? Both their joy and respectful silence exhibit reverence and that the children felt safe and secure in this particular classroom environment to show these feelings. The teacher, by setting up her classroom in this way and allowing the natural world to be part of it, captured the mystery and awe of life that so many of us have felt but maybe could not express. She was able to use these reverent moments and turn them into teaching moments. The birth of the babies occasioned a tie into an age-appropriate lesson in the biology of reproduction, and the demise of the hamster allowed the children to see what a body looks like when it is dead and to understand how it decomposes and returns to the earth.[15]

I worked for a number of years at a retreat center for teachers. Located in the mountains of North Carolina, the center honored teachers through extended hospitality rituals, including such seemingly mundane things as an emphasis on good food and lodging. Teachers expressed that they felt honored by the setting and by the hospitality shown to them.[16] The three buildings of the center all had Cherokee names to honor the land where they were located and to signal what they stood for: *Katusi* (mountain), *Ahysti* (place of exploration), and *Atanto* (human heart or spirit), which the staff roughly translated as: A place in the mountains to explore the human spirit.

The sacralizing of these center buildings through this naming ceremony did not, however, deter some seminar presenters from being irreverent. One presenter in a seminar on democratic education put forth a strongly left-wing ideological position. Many teachers who heard him came from more conservative backgrounds, and any sympathy they might have had for these new and bold ideas was destroyed by the presenter's rigid, self-righteous tone. As the leader of the seminar, I was approached by several teachers who wanted to leave because of the hard-line left ideology and blunt manner of this presenter. This ideologue was not reverent toward the teachers and their own needs for learning in that setting. But then the teachers who shut their ears and their minds and did not try to engage the ideologue were also irreverent. Ideologues of the left or right may be comforted in preaching an idea to others and demanding adherence. Theirs is a smug self-satisfaction that all is good and true, with no need to question further. Reverence for truth teaches us that there is always a need to question and inquire further. But I do not want to let the teachers off as "victims" either. They closed their minds and did not engage the ideologue. These teachers too easily chose not to extend themselves to him to allow what value there may have been in what he said. There is almost always something worthy in what anyone may say. At the very least, these teachers could have learned how to deal with ideologues and even, perhaps, to guard against dogmatism in their own teaching. Both the ideologue and the teachers fell victim to the imposter virtue of false courage, letting it cloud their minds and block the road of free inquiry. Sadly, there are many examples of irreverence in classroom teaching and learning. Recall that irreverence is often attention paid to an imposter virtue, which is a mockery of reverence.

Reverent Educational Leaders

Reverence can also be practical and important for educational leaders such as principals, heads, or superintendents. The most precious component of any practice is not its tools or techniques, though they are no doubt vital, rather it is the skill and virtue of the practitioners themselves. A sense of reverence can inform and enrich the lives of those who lead our schools by invoking appropriate attitudes of awe, wonder, humility, and mutual respect. These attitudes join together the school community into a cohesive whole in service to something greater than us such as justice, love, ideas, ideals, nature's majesty, death, beauty, goodness, or God. Schools are not just places to acquire formal subject matter knowledge, but places to learn how to live a reverent way of life. The expression of reverence in the rituals and ceremonies that unite schools helps to create mutual respect. Educational leaders may rely on reverence without confining it to religion while simultaneously reconciling religious reverence with other forms of reverence for the good of the classroom, school, and community.

Reverence and Leadership Dynamically Intertwined

Wise and provident leaders realize all knowledge is incomplete and therefore listen to others. A reverent leader is not arrogant because she knows she cannot know everything about every situation, but must rely upon followers to provide ideas, ideals, and sometimes, leadership, through which all can learn about a situation and provide solutions to problems. Two short examples, of a custodian and Captain Ahab from Herman Melville's novel, *Moby-Dick,* suffice to illustrate these aspects of reverent leadership.

A Custodian

R. Bruce McPherson tells a story about his work as the director of the residential teacher center I described earlier. One morning, Connie, a custodian at the center, pointed out that two paintings, each of two members of a string quartet, were mounted backwards in the seminar room, so that each pair faced away from the other. McPherson recounted this often as part of the lore and culture of the organization he directed. He writes:

> What Connie was expressing was a sense of wanting all things harmonious, not simply those included in her domain by some filed-away job description. She knew of the NCCAT [The North Carolina Center for the Advancement of Teaching] fetish for client-centered behavior. This was the teachers' seminar room, and something was awry, however subtly. The inclusion of original art in the seminar room, as well as in all the individual sleeping rooms that Connie cleans and arranges, is an institutional value at NCCAT. She felt comfortable initiating change in the realm of values. Her sense of responsibility here was as much moral as practical.[17]

For McPherson the story signifies how everyone in the center, no matter their title or station, possessed or should have possessed a sense of moral responsibility for getting things right. He paid attention and listened to a good suggestion from any member of his staff, and thus exhibited reverence as a leader.

Captain Ahab

A respect between leader and follower is promoted when leaders are reverent, and a reverent leader listens. Captain Ahab, in Herman Melville's novel *Moby-Dick*, does not listen but is bent upon hunting down the white whale that severed his leg. Ahab does not lead his crew, because he does not listen to their concerns, and only uses them for his narrow purpose. The crewmember Starbuck, "endued with a deep natural reverence" and brought up in the Quaker faith where listening is paramount, provides the alternative voice at this point of the novel. He pleads with Ahab, asking him "[w]hy should any one give chase to that hated fish" and passionately imagines his family waiting for him in Nantucket, "[b]ut Ahab's glance was averted, like a blighted fruit tree he shook, and cast his last, cindered apple to the soil."[18] Ahab insists on the irreverent and doomed chase of the whale, taking along all with him to the violent confrontation from which only one man, the novel's narrator Ishmael, survives. When violence breaks out, reverence has fled the scene.[19]

A Higher Authority and Limitations

When leaders appeal to reverence, they appeal to a higher authority than their own. Such attitudes enable everyday technical practice and incite reflection upon the larger beliefs and values that guide that practice by placing the educational leader's actions in a larger context. When a school community and educational leaders have a shared sense of reverence, they can often overcome the disagreements that diversity and difference bring.

Reverence is an encompassing human capacity and a cardinal virtue that, like justice or courage, binds other virtues together. Woodruff suggests that the awe-inspiring object of reverence meets at least one of the following conditions: It cannot be fully controlled or changed by human beings, it cannot ever be fully comprehended, and it is something not created by us even though we may rely upon it to prosper, or it is transcendent in a supernatural sense.[20] Something that satisfies any one of these conditions may involve a reverent sense of individual human limitation that brings a feeling of humility. Examples already mentioned include learning, truth, life, or God. Sometimes the reverent spirit feels something it cannot even name, and sometimes this spirit even expresses itself as humor.

Self-deprecating humor in a leader exhibits reverence, for the leader is drawing attention to his or her limitations. The leader, in so finding humor in personal flaws or limitations, enables the listener to realize that these personal limitations are real. That they are real, and thus connect the leader to those who listen to him or her, is not so limiting as to curb or destroy leadership capacity. Rather, the leader draws people into the vision and plan of where he or she thinks the unit or organization should be going. So much of what passes for "strategic planning" in organizations lacks this extra, but necessary, connection to the leader. Many planning documents founder because they rely merely on "metrics" or other assessment guidelines solely for their enactment and oversight, whereas a strategic plan may be animated and thus carried out through a vital, everyday, vision and practice by a leader and those who cooperate in putting such into action.

Recognizing and acknowledging human limitation with appropriate piety allows members of a community to experience grace. Something greater than their individual egos sustains them. A reverent attitude puts us in our proper place, keeping us from acting like little gods or sinking to the level of beasts. It allows leaders to relax and enjoy that they do not always have to be in charge to lead well. Often they can depend on others in the community such as parents, teachers, and even the students themselves. Some values, like learning to live a better life through reciprocal care and compassion, are so overwhelmingly powerful that we only have to invoke them to bring out expressions of leadership in everyone. Reverence also helps leaders avoid despotism, cruelty, foolishness, and debauchery. It cultivates respect not only for the object of reverence, but also for those who share reverent ideals with us, even when we do not otherwise agree with them.

Reverence is not the same as respect, but is related to it. Respect is part of what one shows while being reverent. Respect thus arises out of reverence. Respect is a feeling or attitude of appreciation, special consideration, or thoughtfulness for others. We may express thoughtful consideration for those with whom we may have profound professional and even religious disagreement if we recognize that we all are equally humbled before a shared mystery or that we pursue many of the same values such as justice, truth, or learning.

Educational leaders should have a sense of awe, wonder, and reverence for the relations that sustain and enhance life. As they do, they are joined to that view Schweitzer saw as the foundation and source of all ethics. These leaders should be devoted to the relations that sustain and enhance the life of students, teachers, parents, and others in the community. These relations are sacred, and once we recognize that we live by the grace of forces we cannot fully comprehend or control, Reverence for Life and recognition of human limitation can complement each other. Strong educational leadership requires many things including appropriate use of science and technology. Reverence for Life brings the insight that we must intelligently employ our rational tools and techniques with empathy and compassion because the goal of educational leadership is to improve the lives of our students, community, and democracy.

We are reverent when we acknowledge our human limitations, including the limits of knowledge. The opposite of such reverent humility is what the classical Greeks called hubris, which expresses itself as an overweening pride and trust in rationality accompanied by a sense of invulnerability such that we need not attend to the thoughts, feelings, and actions of others, especially subordinates. Too often, such hubris accompanies tyranny and tyrannical leadership in society and in our schools.

The Lifeworld, Systemsworld, and Reverent Leadership

Reverence is not something one simply acquires and always has, but like all virtues, it requires a lifetime of continuous practice. Reverence is active, and depends upon shared experience and upon the way we go about working with other individuals in a community. Ceremonies and rituals help bind together reverent communities. While there are many forms of shared experience, rituals can provide exceptionally close connection. Ceremony and ritual are key components of a reverent school culture.

Thomas J. Sergiovanni's distinction, borrowed from Jürgen Habermas, between the "systemsworld" and the "lifeworld" is helpful here.[21] The systemsworld is the realm of rational management, data, test scores, financial statements, and the like. Sergiovanni contrasts that technocratic world with the idea of a lifeworld, that realm of virtue, character, and human connection that gives the tools and techniques of an educational leader deeper and more enduring meaning and value. We must free ourselves from the illusions of disembodied, decontextualized, and dispassionate technique in educating educational leaders and look again at the content and quality of a leader's character. Such techniques are entirely necessary, as we must make sure that systems in schools, such as grade reporting, work smoothly. However, without a vital lifeworld, where a school is connected to human passions, learning that can be imbued with vitality and grace is impossible. A school day becomes a desiccated and often despised routine.

Virtues and virtue ethics take us beyond the ethics of rules and laws and far past the cold, dispassionate, and sometimes even amoral realm of systemsworld regulations and standards. Virtues are embodied predispositions to act that express feeling and emotion. They are about who we are, not just what we believe, and about what we do, not just what we say. A good person just naturally feels like doing the right thing. Reverence is an attitude that influences our thoughts, feelings, and actions. Like other virtues, we acquire reverence by participating in social practices, especially those rituals and ceremonies that connect us to each other and the larger world. Still, reverence is not something we can inculcate or teach directly; like any virtue, we may only acquire it through practice. If we accept that we all have the capacity for reverence, this capacity needs to be practiced and cultivated through a leader's action, and just as significantly, by the ceremonial and ritualistic aspects of schooling that reinforce the capacity to feel reverence.

To the detriment of reinforcing this capacity for reverence, ceremony and ritual rarely receive attention in the education of school leaders. Even today, most of school leadership education concerns systemsworld management issues—buses, beans, and budgets as the saying goes. Too often, the day-to-day work of educational leaders never extends beyond such concerns, vital though they are to the running of a school or district. Exclusive preoccupation with systemsworld demands can cut off educational leaders from the lifeworld, the realm of culture that gives their actions meaning and significance. When technocratic rules and regulations take control, the systemsworld comes to "colonize" the educational leader's consciousness, thereby constraining his or her capacity for sympathetic and compassionate lifeworld response. Educational leaders today not only are occupied with the systemsworld activities of making sure the buses run, but they must respond to strident external testing and accountability mandates. Yet schools need more than bureaucratic management, they need a leader who responds to and fosters the key elements of a school culture, particularly ritual and ceremony.

As a cardinal virtue, reverence ties other virtues together. Reverence for the relations of life and the relations that sustain life is especially relevant for educational leaders who wish to create caring and compassionate school climates. The character of a good educational leader involves many virtues. A very short list would include courage, patience, persistence, being a good listener, and commitment, all encompassed by a self-transcending desire to serve others. A common mistake is to assume virtues are absolute in themselves and exist separate from other virtues. In short, they are something we can simply list and define. Consider, for example, the virtue of courage. Like all virtues, it involves emotions as well as action. Unchecked by compassion, courage may become merely the ferocity of a beast, which destroys one's humanity and quickly turns on those it should serve. Likewise, without intelligence, this virtue becomes foolhardy. True courage knows when the occasion calls for disciplined retreat. Without reflection, courage often allows itself to defend evil against the good. An isolated virtue frequently becomes a vice. Further, vices often pass themselves off as imposter virtues, such as controlling behavior and micromanagement of subordinates in a school or school system.

Sergiovanni makes a strong case for a close connection among many distinct virtues (he mentions integrity, sense of purpose, style, substance, and moral diligence) that define the character of "authentic leadership."[22] While Sergiovanni's idea and his work on the lifeworld of the school and the traits of the virtuous leader are important, the virtue of reverence supplements and enhances Sergiovanni in key ways. First, reverence is a cardinal virtue that helps integrate other virtues of authentic leaders. Second, reverence, like other virtues, belongs to the community, the *polis* in Greek terms, as much as it does an individual. Sergiovanni does a good job of relating the virtues of an individual leader's character with the character of the school or community, or its *ethos*. He is right to insist that education leaders must be "sensitive to the unique values, beliefs, and needs of the followers, when they rely on ideas, values, and well thought-out theories to influence others."[23] Such talk about the values, beliefs, and needs of followers places Sergiovanni's ideas on educational leadership squarely in the camp of moral and cultural approaches. In what follows I discuss two aspects of practical reverence for educational leaders: ceremony and ritual, and shared deliberation.

Reverent educational leadership: Ceremony and ritual

Many leaders do not comprehend or deal adequately with ceremony and ritual in school culture. Even when they acknowledge ceremony and ritual, few recognize the depth of these cultural practices. Ritual may connect people in thought, feeling, and action regarding common ideas and ideals even when they have deep differences in social class, age, ethnicity, race, gender, and sometimes even culture. When we speak of ritual and ceremony, we do not just mean religious worship, sacraments, or liturgy, but also ordinary, everyday customs, procedures, and protocols. Performed with reverence, mundane tasks may invoke a sense of respect for shared traditions, ideas, and ideals. Done properly, common tasks offer occasions for invoking connections among individuals. Ritual and ceremony are powerful means of social unification. Terrence E. Deal and Kent D. Peterson praise "integrative ceremonies" that "provide ways to meld the various social, ethnic, and religious groups in a school."[24] Ritual is an example of practical reverence in concrete educational practice.

Many hold education as a high value even when they disagree on many other fundamental issues of religion and politics. Reverence brings a profound humility before the mystery of life along with recognition of individual limitation and ignorance. Deal and Peterson make much of this "mythic side of a school" that "looms as a school's existential anchor—its spiritual source, the wellspring of cultural traditions and ways."[25] An attitude of reverence recovers the traditions, ceremonies, and rituals of the past into a present that allows the school and its community to imagine and create a richer future. Reverent leaders who can comprehend the school and community's inheritance of generations of learning realize that collective wisdom usually exceeds even the most astute leader. Ceremony and ritual can harvest the greater wisdom of the school and community.

Deal and Peterson assert categorically: "Without ritual and ceremony, any culture will wither and die."[26] They observe that decades of bureaucratic (systemsworld) reform "have managed to sterilize schools of the symbolic acts that help culture survive and thrive."[27] Rituals do transform the commonplace by infusing it with the higher meanings, hopes, and values of the community. Spirit signifies the shared feeling of working together to actualize possibilities, ideas, and dreams within a tradition where the efforts of those who came before sustain us and the success of our efforts will depend on those yet to arrive. So understood, "spirit" has some aspects of immortality that involve telling the story of our lives in a vastly larger and more meaningful context.

Ceremony and ritual formalize embodied actions that invoke feelings and attitudes about beliefs, values, and norms of conduct in those who perform them with commitment. Shared ritual unites participants around notions of the good, true, and right. Ritual may allow its participants to embody intangible, even spiritual, ideas, ideals, and feelings in concrete practice. Such observance aids individuals in forming embodied habits of action that conform to social customs and norms of proper performance. Unquestioned conformity to the social norms of unreflective morality is not, however, a good thing (just think about totalitarian nations). The role of reflection in discerning properly reverent ritual is linked to shared deliberation.

Ceremony can instill habits of right action directed toward the mission and values of such cultural institutions as schools. Deal and Peterson describe one school's annual rite of renewal where "the mission statement is reviewed each fall. It is refined or reworded to match current values.

Then the statement is redone in a new calligraphy by a local artist and signed by everyone. This makes the mission statement alive, vital, connected to everyday experience."[28] Here the acts of deliberation and discussion about an important document are marked by a small gesture of aesthetic pleasure and thoughtfulness.

By participating in common rituals and ceremonies, individuals become part of the larger community wherein they may find their appropriate place and make their contribution. These practices place appropriate limits on leaders, thereby restraining the misuse of power. Ritual and ceremony prevent leaders from becoming tyrants while also protecting the leader from the domination of cliques, cohorts, and even the majority of followers. Both democratic and despotic leaders make use of power, either the power of persuasion or the power of violence. Reverent leaders use power with and for their followers to secure the ideals the society should serve with the least use of brute force possible, while tyrants require oppressive power over their followers and often resort to brute force. Irreverent leaders use ritual wrongly, such as the ghastly displays of racist hatred in Nazi rallies or Klan cross burnings, but distinguishing the difference requires moral deliberation and not simply blanket condemnation.

Wise leaders distribute the leadership function among all who participate in the practice. Sergiovanni speaks highly of "followership" as part of "idea-based leadership" and insists that "when followership is linked to ideas it takes on intellectual and spiritual qualities."[29] Reverent leaders are willing to let others lead when it is best for the overall functioning of the organization. Reverent leaders who have a proper sense of their limitations know they exist by grace in codependent relations with their followers who help sustain them and whom they help sustain for the greater good. Rituals and ceremonies may yet unite a diverse culture, for instance, a pluralistic democracy, in mutual respect and reciprocal admiration regarding the culture's highest ideals (e.g., "life, liberty, and pursuit of happiness" or "all children can learn").

Perhaps the most profound and difficult human limitation to articulate is death. If human beings were immortal, society would not have to reproduce itself biologically or culturally. Education performs the primordial function of initiating the young into culture. Among mortals, if a group cannot reproduce its culturally defining beliefs and ideals in the next generation, the members of that group will vanish. It is this fact that makes debates about education and schooling so understandably intense. It is also why all cultures hold education in high esteem and especially why cultures that have formal school systems value these practices, even if some members of the culture condemn the system's personnel and procedures. The continuity that those who are alive today share with the generations that have gone before and are yet to come is itself worthy of reverence as part of the mystery of existence. It is part of a more general respect. Let us see how this is linked more closely to Schweitzer's ideas, particularly Reverence for Life.

Reverent rituals can acknowledge loss while gathering the passion, compassion, wisdom, and memory necessary for rebirth. Schweitzer's Reverence for Life includes reaching out to what he called, citing *Matthew* 12:33, the "Fellowship of those who bear the Mark of Pain," which for him involves realizing that part of what makes us human is our vulnerability and sensitivity to human suffering.[30] Deal and Peterson provide a simple example depicting "closing rituals" that "furnish the needed support and compassion when things end."[31] These are ways that acknowledge an ending of something important and meaningful, and can be accomplished through sharing a song, taking a group photograph and then signing it, or just enjoying some simple fare over conversation. Similarly, on the last day of any class I say "goodbye" to the room now empty, sometimes uttering students' names and looking around and remembering who was there and what was discussed. I realize that this class will never meet again, and close my eyes for a moment before turning off the lights and leaving.[32]

Reverence is what animates a ritual. Without reverence, a ritual is empty, or worse. Such is dinner time for many American families incessantly on the go with cell phones ringing, soccer practice and homework beckoning, and parents exhausted from the day's work: "Something is missing from these people, something that makes a difference between feeding time and meal time, between a home and a kennel. If you ask them why, they will answer, 'Who has time for family dinner? It's only an empty ritual after all.' True. Without reverence, rituals are empty."[33] Life becomes the spiritually and often physically exhausted iteration of "one damn thing after another" and the lack of reverence leads to this thoughtless, evacuated manner of living.

Likewise, rituals in schools, like the dinner at home, can become simply mere routines again. Rituals disconnected from a school's mission and values fail to summon spirit or to reinforce cultural ties. Indeed, they kill the spirit and break ties. An absence of traditional and vital rituals and ceremonies contributes to "toxic cultures" in schools.[34] In such cultures, leaders and followers lose respect for each other. They no longer know their proper limits and place. Reverence for Life, and the community relations that can sustain it as we have seen in the practices of Schweitzer at his hospital at Lambaréné, dissolve. People only admire themselves. Things become even worse when the rituals become completely empty routine and people even forget the moral rule the routine seeks to capture.

Reverent educational leadership: Shared deliberation and inquiry

Reverence has a critical role in shared rational inquiry. Truth can most inspire a reverential attitude when we realize it transcends our particular lot in the universe. Human beings are not and never will be omniscient. Recognition of human limitation humbles all before the mystery of the unknown and, perhaps, unknowable. Truth can never be the possession of only one person or one leader, however wise. The quest for truth and understanding belongs to every member of the community who answers the call, including those who have come before and those who are yet to come. Reverent leaders are open to learning because they know they are vulnerable to life's shifting contingencies and recognize that even the most assured position is subject to refutation, amendment, and further investigation. Reverence for truth alerts leaders to the permanent possibility of error, and with it, redemptive inquiry.

Reverence for truth and learning requires us to listen carefully to each other. Even the least knowledgeable among us will know something others do not. Those who spend a lifetime, or even only a year or two, in schools are going to learn something, and since every human is a unique individual, it would be most odd if they did not occasionally spot something others have overlooked. The young and those new to an organization are not only its future, but also those most likely to notice what others have become so accustomed to that they can no longer see it. In a pluralistic school, listening becomes especially crucial to learning and growth. We all grow when we are open to new relations with those who are different from us. Educational leaders are no exception, and in fact must work even harder at listening and finding out ideas and information that will enable them to lead effectively. By the nature of their work, leaders can easily become shielded from pluralistic and opposing points of view. These leaders must seek out divergence, while weighing ideas counter to received wisdom and practice, to find the best and most effective course of action. Within the bounds of prudence, an open inquiry, including the sharing of information and opinions, is always to be preferred. Reverence for appropriate persuasion, like reverence for learning, requires that both leaders and followers listen well. While leaders do often know more than their followers, they should nonetheless listen.

Education is the practice of everyone in the community, although, like other esoteric practices, there should be a core of dedicated professionals. Of course, leaders too must know their place. Reverent inquiry allows others, teachers, staff, parents, students, and concerned community members to put the leader in his or her proper place. Deal and Peterson describe many instances of such dispersed deliberation and remark that "the leader must listen for the deeper dreams and hopes the school community holds for the future."[35] Sergiovanni's idea of followership linked to shared ideas, and ideals, has a similar function in distributing deliberation, cultivating leadership, and avoiding tyranny.

A school without reverence for what it knows of its past, or a refusal to learn about it, harms its present and future while a school without reverence for the unknown future betrays its past and its present. Pluralistic democratic learning communities are the best vehicles for deep and enduring change in large part because of their sense of reverent humility, limitation, and respect for the mystery of life and learning, which deprives them of arrogant self-certainty.

Wise inquiry in schools should have its rituals of respect not just for truth and learning, but for each other as well. Thoughtful educational leaders will learn these rituals, preserve them, and, if necessary reinvent them. Reverent deliberation ensures that leaders will not allow meaningful rituals to degenerate into merely empty actions or mechanical systems-world routines that kill a school's spirit and corrupts its values. Even more importantly, it helps protect those within the school from imposter virtues, which is especially important in the case of a cardinal virtue like reverence.

School leaders are essential to the fostering of a school culture that is life-giving rather than life-stultifying. To use the terms of Sergiovanni and Habermas, such a school culture is a morally and aesthetically rich life-world supported rather than dominated or colonized by its bureaucratic systemsworld of procedures and mandates. Practical reverence fostered by a school leader through the languages of ritual, ceremony, and shared deliberation sustains this lifeworld of the school. This practical reverence, so crucial to any leader of a sustained lifeworld, can bring these acts and behaviors into a properly proportioned whole.

Schweitzer and Moral Education

Practical reverence is seemingly paradoxical. It is a way of looking at and being in the world, as well as a set of concrete behaviors. Yet, teachers and educational leaders can carry out and model practical reverence to make schools more just and better places to learn. Schweitzer's insight into and practice of Reverence for Life at his hospital in Lambaréné enlarges the scope of practical reverence by showing ways to connect it materially to other practices in schools. Practical reverence can be situated in a larger more comprehensive sense of moral education relevant to our times, emphasizing narrative and moral imagination.

A Holistic Moral Narrative

Schweitzer's letters to Hélène Bresslau and her letters to him helped as he embarked on what we might call a "moral narrative," where his beliefs and actions are deliberately reconstructed through his writings and behavior to state his moral purpose to the world. Schweitzer was convinced he lived in dark times, where he was combating the spiritual exhaustion of the age, and where he could resign to be a mere "inheritor of the past" as he saw many people doing, particularly his academic colleagues. He saw the age dominated by machine, rather than human, values masking the elements of life essential for humans to live in peace and ethical consideration. This machine age gave us material progress but caused us to lose ourselves spiritually.[1] The way out for Schweitzer is through a commitment to thinking and concomitant action. He sketches this in natural metaphors.

> Just as a tree bears the same fruit year after year and at the same time fruit that is new each year, so must all permanently valuable ideas be continually

created anew in thought. But our age pretends to make a sterile tree bear fruit by tying fruits of truth onto its branches.[2]

The thinking that starts from Reverence for Life is a renewal of elemental thinking. The stream that has been flowing for a long distance underground resurfaces again.[3]

Schweitzer's work is rooted in a holistic sense of morality.[4] Schweitzer works through and joins a number of moral stances that, taken together, are aligned with a number of current metatheoretical stances on morality.

What strikes many people about Schweitzer is the extremity of his commitment that developed in concert with his future wife Hélène Bresslau.[5] His dedication to work at the hospital is remarkable and outside the level of commitment many of us give to causes or beliefs. Thomas Donaldson makes a distinction between minimal duties and actions that may go beyond such minimal duties.[6] If one seeks examples to question the view that everything is reducible to self-interest, then "heroic" (or beyond-minimal-duty) examples are natural, but then the counterargument is often that these "heroes" choose their lifestyles—as though that automatically reveals this choice as just another example of self-interested action. Schweitzer weaves his actions together into a narrative that played out in his letters to his future wife, and his later autobiographical writings. We can examine it as a moral narrative.

Schweitzer consciously created this narrative about the course of his life. Mark Johnson[7] emphasizes the learning of morality as part of our lifetime narrative experience, so that "moral imagination" plays out its hand. Schweitzer takes an even more holistic approach to morality. First of all, he takes seriously important moral principles; second, Schweitzer acts in a way to create a "heroic" lifetime narrative, showing moral imagination and empathy; and finally, he does something pragmatically effective by establishing his hospital and embedding himself in a different culture. He plays out both an implicit and, through his writings, explicit critique of the more hedonistic and materialistic aspects of Western society.

James Rest and his colleagues[8] give us criteria for moral maturity, and these aspects of Schweitzer's character and accomplishments fit well here. In the background to the *Defining Issues Test*, Rest saw that "being a moral person" involves not just being able to identify moral issues and analyze them, but also being able to carry through appropriate moral action. Here, Schweitzer is at the extreme stage of this measure, thinking through the moral issues of his age, educating others about these issues while beckoning them to consider them too, and enacting an educational practice based upon community, hospitality, and leadership.

Schweitzer went to the jungle of Africa with what seems almost like a quaint intent to help. But his resolve and commitment made his work there anything but quaint. He found a brutal climate and difficult terrain, and the lack of funds often hampered his work. Still Schweitzer was able to develop out of the forest there a hospital for the care of the sick.[9] However, it was unlike hospitals that we are accustomed to today, and even for its time, its standards were primitive. Schweitzer developed his hospital, often rebuilding it after leaving for a number of years. The hospital and its rebuilding are comparable to efforts at community education, such as the nineteenth-century settlement homes that made an impact in the lives of people in a particular community. Criticisms Schweitzer received in later life for the conditions of the hospital are comparable to essentialist criticisms of education for hospitality. For curricular essentialists, hospitality is otiose to the learning function of education. Knowledge of the content of a discipline is the goal, and the ecology of teaching and learning is spare: The expert teacher presents content and the student masters it.

We learn from Schweitzer, however, additional, normative lessons. He was drawn to go to Africa out of a need to help others. He sought a way to repay the debt to others, believing one cannot be accepting of what one has, but must give in return. He sensed the enormity of the suffering all around him, from animals to natives in Africa, and resolved to try to alleviate it. He read about the call from the Paris Missionary Society in a pamphlet, for the need for help in what is now Gabon, and his search for a way to serve was over.[10] The call was simple, there was a need, and the way it was worded spoke directly to Schweitzer: "Men and women who can reply simply to the Master's call, 'Lord, I am coming,' those are the people the Church needs."[11]

His family and colleagues surmised that perhaps his career was moving too slowly, or he was unhappy in love. Schweitzer, however, considered himself fortunate to be able to undertake such activities, but not for any sort of personal gain, or sense of heroism. The conviction he had within demanded he follow the path he had chosen:

> Only a person who finds value in any kind of activity and who gives of himself with a full sense of service has the right to choose an exceptional task instead of following a common path. Only a person who feels his preference to be a matter of course, not something out of the ordinary, and who has no thought of heroism but only of a duty undertaken with sober enthusiasm, is capable of becoming the sort of spiritual pioneer the world needs.[12]

So he went, this learned teacher and prolific scholar who had published on Kant, the New Testament, and Bach, this accomplished and fêted organist, to be a simple "jungle doctor."

The Hospital in Lambaréné: Hopes and Concerns

The hospital Schweitzer established in Lambaréné was not orthodox even by early-twentieth-century standards, and current hospitals, with their emphasis on regulation, medical science, and practical intelligence regarding disease and illness, are certainly more advanced. Schweitzer was aware that his hospital lacked the medical technology even available at the time. He accommodated the extended families when they came to the hospital, and knew the value of having the family and others there to support the healing. While we now know the value of such practices, we don't practice them as fully as Schweitzer was able to with his small hospital.

He made do with the supplies that were available and had to constantly raise funds to keep the hospital running. Many of the instruments and supplies were old or out of date. Sanitary practices were not modern, and shocked a number of visitors. John Gunther's 1955 book *Inside Africa*[13] solidified a view about Schweitzer that may be one factor in the demise of his influence or recognition. Schweitzer was dismissed as kindly but misguided and even racist, a physician who did not use modern methods of medicine or even rudimentary sanitation. Others noted differently, that Schweitzer worked among those in the hospital daily. Several times the hospital had to be rebuilt, and he participated. He built trust within the community, but also expected all who came for services to contribute.[14]

So what was this "hospital," so indelibly associated with its founder who, aside from brief periods in Europe to raise money, spent over 50 years there? Calling what Schweitzer started in Lambaréné a hospital does confuse the issue for many of us, so accustomed are we to modern, technically assisted healthcare. J. F. Montague believed such a word is a poor descriptor for what Schweitzer built and accomplished there. The facility on the banks of the Ogooué was a communal effort involving extended families as support for the "patients," where Schweitzer saw his task was to relieve pain, but not to redo lives.[15]

Montague further asserts in stiff prose "Lambaréné was primarily an experiment in humanitarian effort using the medical avenue of approach."[16] Norman Cousins agrees that Lambaréné was more like a "clinical community" where a larger, social understanding of healing was enacted and hospitality practiced.[17] What follows is a brief account of two major stages of the hospital, namely, how it was established and the reaction to its operation by people outside of it who may have made only short or fact-finding visits.

In the Academy Award–winning documentary about Schweitzer by Jerome Hill and Erica Anderson, candid shots of the hospital, and the living quarters of patients, show what John Gunther and others had experienced and reported. Schweitzer had the living quarters constructed so entire families could come and be part of the healing of the patient. Beds were made with ample room underneath to store pots and other cooking supplies. Animals ran freely, and cooking fires burned in front of these quarters. Simply put, the hospital was hospitable, casual, and inviting to its guests, as it replicated in some degree the cultural context from which they came. Hospitality here and elsewhere means being open and welcoming to the other. Such a welcome leaves open the possibility of learning from that other. Like a hospital, a classroom too can be hospitable or inhospitable. Locked doors and other signs of lack of trust undermine the learning experience.[18]

Ironically though, these efforts to create a safe environment may signal otherwise, that trust and calm order are not present and must be somehow artificially created. Teachers and administrators in these circumstances must make extra effort to overcome these signals, and often will find they are conflicted in doing so. The shootings at Colorado's Columbine High School in 1999 alerted all educators to be vigilant for the signs of underlying discontent or even terror while at the same time attending to learning.

Lessons from Lambaréné

Areas of education that focus now upon the school as part of the community and school/community interaction can benefit from a consideration of Schweitzer's efforts to establish his hospital/clinic/healing community in Lambaréné. The hospital can be compared to a variety of innovative social practices in education from that time, such as Jane Addams' Hull House, and to current efforts to incorporate cultural practices in schooling. The lifeworld[19] practices of Lambaréné were well-established and can provide a model for analysis by other efforts at community education. Other educational practices from that time, such as the establishment of community centers by external authority in the Gary Indiana Plan of 1909–1915, show that a lasting effort to develop a community-based education must take into account some of the factors evident in the Lambaréné hospital.

In making these connections between Schweitzer's work and other endeavors, I want to stress core features of his personality. Schweitzer's emphasis upon positive change was enacted through what we in universities now call engagement. Such deeds are fueled by a deep and unswerving resolve by Schweitzer, based upon a sober view of what he saw as a decayed and decaying civilization, and the need to make a personal statement to the world. This homogeneity of purpose within Schweitzer serves as an ideal for measuring one's own actions.

We live now in a culture of accountability and bottom-line results. School leaders and teachers are under increasing pressure to improve results and meet mandated standards. At the same time, many of us do not want to leave children behind. While accountability measures weigh heavily upon schools, Schweitzer points to issues that are deeper and can generate meaning to serve as an antidote to the deadening within education that occurs with emphasis upon standards and accountability. Schweitzer's educational contribution, and particularly his hospital, can be viewed through lenses of engagement, environmental awareness, hospitality, and community. Recent efforts toward such a model, inspired by Schweitzer, are discussed in the context of a counter to accountability measures in our schools.

Schweitzer's work in Africa and his writings provide rich seams of thought to mine for a philosophy of education that can both inspire and empower the educational process in our schools. First, from his answer to the question, "What should we humans educate ourselves to be and to do?" Schweitzer's philosophy of life and his actions show us that education should teach us how to serve others and our world, rather than be mere consumers. second, through an interpretation of his principle "Reverence for Life," Schweitzer offers an understanding of our environment as more than home and neighborhood, as Nature itself, an organic, living source of all that has value; and finally, education in learning the art of hospitality helps us to form meaningful, respectful, fulfilling communities of learning.

Schweitzer's Moral Education

Schweitzer made an early commitment not to harm living things and to live in accordance with the demands of a conscience and a sense of duty toward others. He was sensitive to the suffering of downtrodden humans and hapless animals, a sensitivity he recounts many times, in particular the defining incident with the bird and slingshot discussed in Chapter 1. This significant moment in Schweitzer's childhood, and other experiences recalled in his *Memoirs*, became his own earned and genuine moral education. What he observed helped to educate him about what philosophers the world over call "the Good," that which funds human life with compassion, decency, justice, and grace. Schweitzer's reflections upon his experiences drove home the lesson.

Schweitzer, the son of a Lutheran pastor, was considered a "hopeless dunce in school until he saw the point of study."[20] He questioned the works of the great philosophers, and contemporary ones, such as Marx, Freud, and Nietzsche, for the basis of ethics that he would not find, to his satisfaction, until later in Africa. He loved playing the organ, wrote a seminal work on Bach, and would later earn money for his African hospital by giving concerts in Europe. He focused on the life of Jesus of Nazareth, finding fault in previous scholarship, and wrote a study of the "historical Jesus." Even though he was a successful scholar and musician, he decided in his early twenties that he would occupy himself with scholarship and music only until the age of 30, after which he would devote himself to a life of service, having evolved toward that with the help of his soul mate and future wife, Hélène. Such is Schweitzer's answer to Descartes' famous dictum, *cogito ergo sum*—I think therefore I am:

> Descartes started on this basis. But he built an artificial structure by presuming a person knows nothing and doubts all, whether outside himself or within. And in order to end doubt, he fell back on the fact of consciousness: I think. Surely, however, that is the stupidest primary assumption in all philosophy! Who can establish the fact that he thinks, except in relation to thinking something? And what that something is, is the important matter.[21]

Through his life of action, Schweitzer thought about "something" and lived a life of action. He became what the philosopher Ann Hartle calls Michel de Montaigne: a "great-souled man without pride."[22] The comparison is apt. Hartle sees Montaigne as building upon the Aristotelian term *megalopsuchia*, sometimes translated as magnanimity or great-souledness.[23] Aristotle had said that "magnanimity is the virtue that disposes us to do good to others on a large scale"[24] For Hartle, Montaigne develops a sense of Christian magnanimity, blending classical great-souledness with Christian humility. This same humility is evident in Schweitzer's magnanimity toward helping others on a more sustained and larger scale than Montaigne ever did.

Schweitzer's resolve to serve others in the manner he chose as a young man, namely, medicine, did not fail him, though he had doubts and setbacks. He and his wife were prisoners of war during World War I. When they returned to Africa years later in 1924, the hospital was dilapidated and untended and had to be rebuilt. As he was determined to be at his best and to live according to his principles, so too can such a principled life serve to call others, including educators, to be not only at their best, but to reflect and scrutinize life choices. He encouraged others to "find their own Lambaréné" in their lives and communities, where they could construct and enact their own moral narratives.

Such a moral narrative may help us learn what it means to be an educated person. Narrative has unity and such union is sorely needed in order to build identity. Teachers, teacher educators, school leaders, and others should focus on teaching and modeling ways for children to see their lives as a narrative unity, so that young people might develop the skills of reflecting deeply and effectively upon the many choices and dilemmas that life presents. Early experiences, such as Schweitzer's observations about animals, grounded his later moral reflections and helped him to understand morality in a holistic way. Such a cohesive and unified vision of one's life is what educators can help young people to work toward, to offset the many ways that one's being is wrenched apart into the discrete roles of consumer, market-driven producer, spectator, and so forth. Schweitzer's construction of such a moral narrative yields a three-part educational legacy: education for service; education for environmental awareness; and education for hospitality and community.

Education for Service

For Schweitzer, service was a calling toward a very simple task, where a "human being is always a human being, always someone who has a right to the assistance and sacrifice of his fellow men."[25] Service for Schweitzer is selfless and constant, and looking toward the needs of the other, whether that is a human being or another living thing. It is an emptying of the ego and a facing outward toward others. Schweitzer saw how egoistic needs could be destructive, such as in Nietzsche's philosophy or in the colonialism that rapaciously took resources from Africa. He reached out to what he called the "Fellowship of those who bear the Mark of Pain,"[26] realizing that what makes us human is precisely our vulnerability and sensitivity to the suffering of others. This condition calls us to join others to try to make a better world. Service for Schweitzer thus is an ontological venture, where one brings about a new reality through other-regarding action.

We who teach, work toward the betterment of our students and communities. And, too, teachers may respond to what David T. Hansen terms the "call to teach," to this idea of a pedagogical vocation which is "a mirror into which all prospective and practicing teachers might look . . . that invites teachers to self-scrutiny and self-reflection."[27] This mirror is not merely reflective, but beckons one toward expansive and high ideals, in that it "calls (teachers) to be at their best when in the presence of their students. It urges them to act, at a minimum, as if their work were a vocation, regardless of whether they in fact view it as such."[28] Reflection on Schweitzer's resolve to serve humanity leads us to ask why educators invest in and devote themselves to prompting knowledge and self-awareness in others.

When Schweitzer decided to leave his successes in scholarship and music at age 30 and enter medical school in October 1905, he too was called to act in service. In a sermon just before his thirtieth birthday in January 1905, he contrasted what he saw as the selfless work of missionaries to a European colonialist culture that "speaks so piously of human dignity and human rights and then disregards this dignity and these rights of countless millions and treads them underfoot, only because they live overseas or because their skins are of different color or because they cannot help themselves."[29] He made committed *action* his means of cultural and spiritual regeneration:

> But was I to teach [in a seminary] that which I did believe? If I did so, would this not bring pain to those who had taught me? Faced with these two questions, I decided that I would do neither. I decided that I would leave the seminary. Instead of trying to get acceptance for my ideas, involving painful controversy, I decided I would make my life my argument. I would advocate the things I believed in terms of the life I lived and what I did. Instead of vocalizing my belief in the existence of God within each of us, I would attempt to have my life and work say what I believed.[30]

For Schweitzer, it was a turn toward action and to others, a turn away from the scholarly life by itself that defined his view of service. It was not just the acquisition and consumption of knowledge, but rather the formation of a passionate commitment toward the specific path and goal of service toward others based upon a selfless duty toward other human beings, indeed toward all living things. Schweitzer was determined to find a thought that would ground and animate all thinking and action, especially his own. He struggled to be not merely part of an end-of-century pessimism, where he "felt like someone who has to replace a rotten boat that is no longer seaworthy with a new and better one, but does not know how to proceed."[31] Schweitzer sought a bedrock principle upon which to affirm civilization and to make it whole from the inside out, rather than presuming society should be manipulated through the application of tools from science and technology.

As Schweitzer established his new hospital in Lambaréné in the spring of 1913, his mind was engaged in an active quest for this grounding principle. Reverence for Life is the principle upon which Schweitzer would base his entire thought and action in Africa. He achieved this by seeking what was elemental and foundational. Unlike an indubitable foundation on which to build knowledge that is the dream of philosophers such as Descartes and Husserl, however, Schweitzer's principle of Reverence for Life moves one *outward* to a connection with a larger whole that is Nature and other living beings. He recognizes existence is "unfathomably mysterious." Yet there is reciprocity with other living things, in granting the same kind of feeling toward oneself that one feels toward another. This is what Schweitzer means when he says that "(man) experiences that other life in his own."[32] Reverence for Life extends to Nature, so that *all* living creatures and organisms share this inherent right for "reverence" for the very quality of possessing life. By observing Reverence for Life, Schweitzer wanted to help individuals "think more deeply and more independently."[33] He believed purpose and motive must be found by each individual, beyond the consumerist culture that threatens the development of such independent thinking and being. This "spirit of the age" forces people into a kind of herd, so that they are not thinking for themselves but want others to do this for them, that "in spite of his great technological achievements and material possession, he is an altogether stunted being, because he makes no use of his capacity for thinking."[34]

Schweitzer valued freedom of thought above even a slavish and funda-mentalist application of Reverence for Life.

> From the natives I buy a young fish eagle, which they have caught on a sand-bank, in order to rescue it from their cruel hands. But now I must decide whether I shall let it starve, or whether I shall kill a certain number of small fish every day in order to keep it alive. I decide upon the latter course. But every day find it rather hard to sacrifice—upon my own responsibility—one life for another.[35]

Here he acknowledges that his freedom of thought comes with a dilemma of responsibility that is often hard to bear. He makes a choice based on a hierarchy of values but does so with difficulty and regret.

Education for Environmental Awareness

Education for environmental awareness is grounded upon the realization that human beings are part of the world and not in dominion over it. This false or deluded sense of dominion has led to exploitation of nonrenew-able natural resources at the expense of sustained living. Such dominion is ultimately a lack of respect for one's surroundings. The source of this lack of respect is seeing human beings as apart from, rather than part of, the natural environment. Schweitzer's principle of Reverence for Life helps to overcome this cleavage between humans and the world. At times he expounded this view in a way many would find extreme:

> You are walking along a path in the woods. The sunshine makes lovely patterns through the trees. The birds are singing, and thousands of insects buzz happily in the air. But as you walk along the path, you are involuntarily the cause of death. Here you trod on an ant and tortured it; there you squashed a beetle; and over there your unknowing step left a worm writhing in agony. Into the glorious melody of life you weave a discordant strain of suffering and death. You are guilty, though it is no fault of your own. And, despite all your good intentions, you are conscious of a terrible inability to help as you would like to. Then comes the voice of the tempter: Why torture yourself? It is no good. Give up, stop caring. Be unconcerned and unfeeling like everybody else.[36]

Schweitzer believed that as long as humans believe that they have a natural right to superiority and dominion over the rest of the natural world, a true ethic of Reverence for Life cannot be achieved. One of the lessons from taking Reverence for Life seriously is environmental awareness.

Such awareness has been a curricular aim, albeit on the fringe of practice, for over 30 years. Well-known texts at the beginning of the current environmental movement, such as Rachel Carson's *Silent Spring* (dedicated to Schweitzer) and Aldo Leopold's *Sand County Almanac* alerted us to the fragility of the planet and our place in it. The stresses upon the biosphere, due to increased industrialization coupled with rapid population increases and continued use of fossil fuels, have not been met with a proactive public policy. One way to strengthen an awareness of this crisis is making the connection between Schweitzer's Reverence for Life principle and John Dewey's thoughts about Nature, as I did earlier in connecting Deweyan natural piety. This connection has not been made though it is powerful and may result in action beyond mere awareness of the environmental crisis.

In Chapter 1 of *Experience and Nature*, Dewey discusses what he calls "*the* philosophic fallacy" regarding Nature.[37] The primary, or ordinary, experience one has with Nature shows us its mutability, and even, as Dewey states, what Santayana calls its "exuberance." The fallacy of philosophers is to try to convert Nature into something quite other: permanent, unchanging, eternal, a thing rather than a process. This fallacy is taken even further when Nature becomes merely a commodity to be used by us, such as the timber on the Ogooué River near Lambaréné in Schweitzer's time or the oil in the Gulf of Mexico today.

Dewey argued against dualism in its many guises: mind and body, individual and society, content and form. Yet he recognizes that our "intricate relation" with Nature involves not only a recognition of instability, change, volatility, and exuberance, but also that these qualities spawn our yearning for permanence. This leads us to philosophical inquiry. We see impermanence, and strive for a kind of understanding, creating art and culture. The fallacy is in the fixation of thought and of Nature as split apart from each other, and not recognizing the dynamism and dialectic of this process. A typical human wish is to control and eliminate change, to fix a process to a stable and permanent essence that we can then fully and permanently understand and even control. Dewey shows how only a provisional fixity can be achieved in cultural, especially artistic, production. The works of art, of culture, are simply structures by which to view a changing reality. And, in any case, these objects themselves, subject to endless interpretation, are never fixed and inert in an absolute sense.

Schweitzer was unsuccessful in meeting Dewey during his only trip to the United States in 1949 to give the Goethe address in Aspen, Colorado. Yet we know that Dewey and Schweitzer read each other's work, and can surmise that they would have had this argument against such dualisms in common. Schweitzer's daily challenges with the volatility, impermanence, and certainly the exuberance of a lush tropical Africa illustrate Dewey's concept of "a changing reality." Within that dynamic world of Nature, Reverence for Life grounded Schweitzer's entire philosophy and his daily work. Once, an antelope fawn was brought to Schweitzer after some local hunters had unsuccessfully tried to trap its mother. Schweitzer named it Léonie and nursed it on a bottle. Léonie and another antelope, Théodore, would then accompany him on strolls to the river and lick the salty sweat off his arm. For Schweitzer, reverence was physical as well as spiritual. He also had a down-to-earth sense of reverence for others with whom he might disagree, an attitude that allowed him to be patient and compassionate in trying circumstances: "I still hear the Doctor's words when faced with someone difficult. He would always say in Alsatian, 'Weisch, mir mien ne ewe vertraje,' which means, 'You know how it is, we have to put up with this.' His point was to tolerate and accept the other person."[38] Thus, Schweitzer's philosophy of Reverence for Life touched all aspects of his life and was extended to all living beings. Schweitzer transformed his philosophical idea of Reverence for Life into action at his hospital at Lambaréné, as well as in the work of countless others who remember his legacy. By meeting Nature mostly on its own terms, as Schweitzer did each day in his African hospital, one may be prevented from making Nature into what some of us hope it can be, but cannot unless we wish to destroy it, namely, a lifeless, manipulated commodity.

The pedagogical implications for viewing Nature in the related ways of Dewey and Schweitzer are important. In *The Quest for Certainty*, Dewey spoke about the common educational practice of "reduplication."[39] Reduplication occurs when one applies without attention some principle or bit of information, merely mimicking what has already been created. Dewey said this could be no more than a pale copy, like a photograph (taken as a snapshot and not with artistic intention). The practice of reduplication in many of our schools today supports what Dewey calls "*the* philosophic fallacy," and by extension, the unthinking, unaware, and even fearful manipulation of Nature. In a quest for certainty enacted every day in schools, the common practice of "teaching to the test," or learning atomized factual information about a topic with no connection to an imaginative or useful application, is this same reduplication. A child's mouthing or scribbling platitudes about one's country or flag pales in importance to that same child learning how to resolve conflict by discussing these differences among others in a respectful, democratic arena. Recognizing Nature in its ordinariness, as well as with an awe-filled reverence coupled with a sense of responsibility, as Dewey points to and Schweitzer exemplifies, should be one of the ends of an environmentally aware practice in education. We would do well to teach our students, and show them by example, that we are stewards of our environment with a moral duty to live in harmony with, and preserve our natural world, rather than exploiting and destroying it. Schweitzer's Reverence for Life, coupled with Dewey's natural piety, can be our model for this endeavor.

Education for Hospitality and Community

Schweitzer's work can teach us about the importance of hospitality and community in teaching and learning. These two ends of schooling are often pushed aside or forgotten. The culture of accountability and bottom-line results that pervades our schooling do not lead to the desired ends, namely enhanced learning. Instead, school leaders and teachers are under increasing pressure to improve students' test scores and meet mandated standards and not leave any children behind. Schweitzer's work points to deeper and more generative meanings for educational practice that can be an antidote to the deadening that occurs too often with the emphasis upon external mandated standards and accountability. His hospital in Lambaréné, designed and operated to emphasize *hospitality* and *community* to its patients and their families, provides an example for an invitational practice of learning within education.

Hospitality is something beyond the "hospitality industry" or what Henri Nouwen calls "[a] soft sweet kindness, tea parties, bland conversations, and a general atmosphere of coziness."[40] Hospitality is rather the activity of receiving another person, listening to that person, and being open to what that person has to say. Here there is often a reversal of roles accompanied by a humbling experience: "In teaching, when you listen to the student, the student becomes the teacher."[41] Such listening to others becomes part of the pedagogy of hospitality. Max van Manen calls this *tact* in teaching,[42] where you are present in mind, body, and soul for the student. This is in contrast to a detached and instrumentalist view of teaching where the student is a receptacle to be filled with knowledge, or a chunk of raw material to be worked on in making a finished "product." At the hospital in Lambaréné, Schweitzer did not try to change native customs, but adapted Western medical practices so that they would work alongside more traditional modes of African healing. He was not perfect, and can be faulted for not learning more about native customs, languages, and other cultural practices. Yet he listened well to what were the needs of his patients and their families, and tried to provide for their comfort in healing.

Schweitzer was savagely criticized late in life for the backwardness of his hospital. But for him, it was a "Garden of Eden,"[43] operating more like a healing community.[44] Today's hospitals, with their emphasis on regulation, cutting-edge medical science, and the intellectual understanding of disease and illness may be more proficient in diagnosis and treatment of illness, but they simply do not match the holistic and hospitable environment that Schweitzer enacted at Lambaréné. He purposely allowed the hospital to develop as an African village, because he saw that the *communal* aspects of African life, such as allowing patients and their accompanying families to cook their own meals, were a healing resource alongside traditional Western medicine. Having the extended families of patients present and engaged in work around the hospital, such as tending gardens, also was shrewd management of resources, in that many more patients could be served. Thus, the practical purposes of affirming the members of that native culture, which include healing and cost benefits, were joined to a moral purpose, namely, affirming connection among members of that culture, and preserving life.

Allowing the entire family, and their animals, to accompany the sick person, appalled some visitors. Schweitzer's medical practice has been criticized as not only unhygienic and backward, but patronizing and colonialist. W. E. B. Du Bois faults Schweitzer for not realizing "what modern exploitation means, of what imperial colonialism has done to the world" but goes on to say that "he deserves every tribute that we can give him for trying to do his mite, his little pitiful mite, which in a sense was but a passing gesture, but perhaps in the long run will light that fire in Africa which will cleanse that continent and the world."[45] While Schweitzer's attitude toward African societies and culture is controversial, it should be mentioned that he was well aware of the destructive and intrusive aspects of European culture in Africa, from the psychological to the material: "The cheap enamelled (sic) ware has driven out the solid, home-made wooden bucket, and round every negro (sic) village there are heaps of such things rusting in the grass."[46] And he was well aware of the rapacious exploitation of timber in his part of Africa.

While Schweitzer may not have fully comprehended the impact of colonial practices, his work reveals ethical commitment more than ethnocentric blindness, as Du Bois notes. He understood the harm embedded in colonialism, witnessing first-hand the effects of alcohol and infectious diseases upon native populations. Yet, Schweitzer was a man of his times, thinking that Europeans had a natural authority over African natives. I acknowledge his bias and certainly do not laud it, but like Du Bois, want to point beyond this limitation. Schweitzer's example shows how each person can build narrative structure into their moral lives whereby they can increasingly move beyond cultural prejudices and "take in more and more of the human tapestry into which we are all woven, despite countless differences."[47] His later writings about the danger of nuclear weapons show that he was not driven by ideology but built upon this ethical commitment that he developed through continuous reflection upon his work throughout his life. This reflection was linked to practical concerns in service of others, a concern that had evolved to encompass the global community. While Schweitzer expressed grave concern about global conflict in his Nobel Peace Prize lecture, he used the funds from the prize to build a facility for lepers near his hospital, *Village Lumière* or "Village of Light."

Many hospitals and schools are apart from the communities they serve. A rural school near where I used to live sits amidst vast cornfields, and every person going to that school, student, staff, and teacher, must get there by vehicle. In the inner city, schools are often locked down, and students must enter through guarded doors, watched by surveillance cameras and inspected by metal detectors. This separateness is hardened by procedures aimed at a standardization of practice, whether it is for the treatment of disease or the learning of mathematics, that can be replicated anywhere. Schweitzer's hospital grew out of an organic relationship to the people it served, as well as the particular characteristics of its setting in what is now Gabon. It is similar to a variety of innovative social practices in education, from settlement homes in the late nineteenth and early twentieth century, such as Jane Addams's Hull House in Chicago, to current efforts to incorporate cultural practices in schooling and make schools more caring and homelike. Jane Roland Martin's "schoolhome" does not envision school as "a special kind of production site" where standards must be met and quality control exerted, nor does it "picture young children as raw material, teachers as workers who process their students before sending them on to the next station on the assembly line, or curriculum as the machinery that over the span of twelve of so years forges America's young into marketable products."[48] Rather, she sees the model being Maria Montessori's *Casa dei Bambini*, where one is comfortable and secure, "at home" in a place that supports learning.[49] In such institutions, hospitality is thus not a byproduct of centrally mandated arrangements, but is the part of the culture, just as it was and is at the Albert Schweitzer Hospital. Just as such core beliefs and practices animate healing, so do they animate learning. Schweitzer realized that he had to be open to the native culture in which he built his hospital and practiced medicine in order to be effective in his work.

Norman Cousins tells the story of a student in France in 1957 who when asked on an examination to name the person who represented the best hope for the culture of Western Europe, replied, "It is not in any part of Europe. It is in a small African village and it can be identified with an eighty-two year old man."[50] While the line of influence from Schweitzer to our current educational practices may not be as direct, it can be just as powerful. Schweitzer urged educators to "instill in your students an awareness that they are on this earth to help and serve others."[51] Teachers sometimes despair of reaching every student and making a difference. School leaders feel constricted by conflicting mandates of accountability and finding ways to enable every child to succeed and not be left behind. Teacher educators wonder if what they discuss in our colleges and universities will make a mark on teacher candidates, and be transformed into their own reflective practices. Schweitzer realized that such work may be modest at times, but it certainly is no less important than heroic deeds. As Robert Payne notes: "Once Goethe had written: "In our younger days we were sure we could build palaces for mankind. With experience we learn that the most we can do is to clean up their dunghills." Schweitzer was determined to clean up the dunghills."[52] The rich example of Schweitzer's life and work serves, much as Hansen's idea of vocation as a mirror, to call us to reflect upon our own motivations to teach and learn. And, too, Schweitzer's philosophy of Reverence for Life shows us ways to teach others about Nature in its ordinariness and majesty, so that we can live and abide in its midst in a better and more accommodating way.

The once modest hospital in Lambaréné—inauspiciously begun in a chicken coop in 1913—is now a significant healthcare center managed by an international consortium of Europeans, Americans, and Gabonese, with a new Research Laboratory and success in reducing the impact of malaria in the region. But most importantly, the hospital has maintained the "Schweitzer spirit" for nearly a century with an attitude of service, a respect for Nature, and a welcoming spirit to those who come to be healed. Just imagine the consequences of a similar spirit taking hold in present-day classrooms. "Truth has no special time of its own. Its hour is now." Schweitzer said. As we listen to his truth, we hear a full life of commitment speaking to the present and the future. Emboldened by this example, we might even envision an educational philosophy based on the simple humanity of Reverence for Life.

Establishing a medical facility in the interior jungle of equatorial Africa was a huge and daunting endeavor. This would be a difficult task with a crew and sufficient supplies and equipment. Schweitzer had neither of these when he started his work in 1913. Several times he had to rebuild the hospital, most extensively during 1924–1927, and moved it completely to a new location in 1925.[53] The first task was to establish contact and gain confidence. He accomplished this by taking part in the physical work needed to clear the grounds and build the hospital. Schweitzer took part in the clearing and construction himself. Photographs of him working with others to erect the buildings prove his support of a community of practice. This image, though, along with accounts and photographs of him playing a piano that was specially equipped for the humid climate, contribute to the Schweitzer myth of course, but testify to his extraordinary range of interests sustained under adverse circumstances, within his unwavering commitment to serve others.

8

Icon, Scoundrel, Prophet, Paradigm? A Recovery Project for Schools

Schweitzer established his hospital on a river's edge in Gabon. He ministered to the ill there, quietly going about his work as a dutiful disciple of Jesus, until the plaudits of the world came to him. He accepted these accolades with grace, all the while clad in colonial white, and without interruption continued to dispense wisdom and medicine in the harsh jungle. That is all part of the Schweitzer myth that has been constructed about him, embellished by the ages but with a basis. For now, let us bracket these arguably mythic qualities and analyze this image. The kindly jungle doctor is part of the Schweitzer legend that has been abetted by a number of admirers over the years. Just as the film *Le Grand Blanc de Lambaréné*[1] discussed below largely misses the point of his devotion, so too does a hagiographic depiction of this remarkable person prevent us from seeing his lasting contribution in its full light. Schweitzer was of course a multi-faceted and complicated figure. He has been lionized and worshipped, criticized and mocked. If we are to use Schweitzer's lessons for education, it would be better if we examined those achievements on the Ogooué River in Gabon in the first half of the last century, and what he says about these achievements, more clearly.

A Recovery Project

In previous chapters, I sketched Schweitzer's life and background. I described and analyzed the conditions under which his idea of Reverence for Life came forth, and attributed part of the foundation for that revelation to his long friendship and subsequent marriage to Hélène

Bresslau. The Schweitzer myth and image come from later in life, and should be cleared to one side if only temporarily in order to begin to understand his lasting significance for education.

This recovery project[2] starts with images of Schweitzer constructed when he was an old man, portrayed as the "kindly jungle doctor among the natives." The sanitized and hagiographic Schweitzer comes to us largely through accounts such as that of Norman Cousins and the 1957 Academy Award–winning documentary, *Albert Schweitzer*.[3] There is a counterimage of Schweitzer proposed in a more recent 1995 film, *Le Grand Blanc de Lambaréné*. Each film gives us insight into the Schweitzer myth and each is a distorted image of the man, valuable though as a way of gauging Schweitzer's overall contributions, but not so much the educational value of this legacy.

These two films help get a discussion of the Schweitzer myth off the ground, but reasons for the myth deserve critique. Here both metaphors of a recovery and an excavation project[4] are useful. Through a reconsideration and analysis, new and other meanings will emerge, permitting a consideration of whether Schweitzer is an educational prophet, and related to this, a consideration of him as a paradigm of his age. The thoughts of David Purpel, Karl Jaspers, and Jeffrey Ayala Milligan guide these examinations.

Two Films about Schweitzer

Albert Schweitzer

The film *Albert Schweitzer* by Jerome Hill and Erica Anderson came out in 1957 and received the 1957 Academy Award for Best Documentary. It begins with a scrolled text about understanding of the life of Schweitzer. We learn that the filmmakers spent six years of hardship and strain making the film while in Africa, though the first part of the film takes place in Schweitzer's boyhood home, Günsbach, in Alsace on the border of France and Germany. Schweitzer agreed to the filming on the condition that it not appear during his lifetime, though the film eventually came out seven years before his death.

The director Jerome Hill starts with brief footage of Schweitzer himself, taken from a dramatic low angle to foreground his commanding visage and leonine swept white hair against a plain sky. This image, combined with the solemn text that precedes it, signals that this will be a respectful, possibly hagiographic documentary. Following this image are quite different, even whimsical, scenes of seemingly carefree African natives getting water from a pump, complete with sprightly background music. The contrast between the commanding visage of Schweitzer and the "happy natives" couldn't be starker. From there, brief context-setting scenes follow, and we are transported to where Schweitzer came from, the village of Günsbach, idyllically portrayed as a simple and small town, nestled in a valley and almost timeless in its appeal, as local people harvest grapes and go about their manual agricultural tasks. We are reminded by the narrator that Schweitzer considers this his home, too, though he has spent little of his adult life here. At the train station, Schweitzer arrives, an elderly man, riding alone and without fanfare back to Günsbach. The narrator intones that he rode third class, because there is no fourth class. The film calls upon us to ask why Schweitzer would give up his seemingly idyllic life in Alsace, as we see in loving and respectful detail the village of Günsbach, and the timeless way in which people still live.

But Schweitzer was not to spend time here in Alsace on a holiday, without penitential labor. He works on his correspondence, sees his family, greets neighbors, and hearkens back to the time when he had to leave his "carefree" childhood to go out to school. Yet his childhood was anything but carefree, as text from Schweitzer states that even then he did not know the "sheer joy of being alive" but rather appeared content, hiding a great deal of turmoil inside. What prompts an inner soul-searching is the suffering he sees all around, in seemingly routine activities of Nature, such as insects feeding on each other. An emaciated feral dog signals the even more disturbing suffering of animals. At night, the young Schweitzer prayed for all living things, not just humans, and slowly developed an ethical consciousness that he attributes to these childhood lessons. Early life is captured best in the episode of him going off with a friend to shoot birds with a slingshot, dramatically portrayed and faithfully rendered according to Schweitzer's own words with his grandson portraying the young Albert.

When we see Schweitzer in Lambaréné in this film, the contrast with Günsbach is clear. He is among others, at work as a medical doctor. There is timelessness to Lambaréné as there is to the Günsbach scenes, as clock time does not run the daily business of the hospital here on the banks of the Ogooué River. There are common meals, signaled to all by a peal of a central, hand-rung bell. Patients come with a wide variety of ailments that we do not see typically in modern society, such as strangulated hernias and leprosy. Schweitzer said that he established the hospital to atone for the suffering caused in the world by those more privileged than him, and that the "Lord Jesus" had sent him, the good doctor, and this lord would take away the pain and suffering.

We see entire families arrive with the sick. They are received openly no matter how many there are. This is central to the healing process. The families come laden with cooking utensils, and build fires outside the lodgings for their daily meals. Goats and other animals roam freely about the compound, and smoke from campfires is constant. Though fruit trees are plentiful and we learn that Schweitzer regarded the hospital as a "garden of Eden," he and his group of workers tried to stretch resources and live within their means. Shipping cards were reused for patient identification cards, and the narrator tells us solemnly that "everything at the hospital had value, nothing was thrown away," though other evidence of this conservation is not shown so directly. Instead, we see and hear about the unceasing construction of the hospital: metal roofs are bought for the leper compound with money from the Nobel Peace Prize, while wood from okoumé trees is harvested and used to build the walls of the buildings because of its obdurate strength and durability.

The narrator informs us that though Schweitzer was aware of modern medical practices, he chose to avoid newer technical devices as they proved to be expensive, hard to keep up, and removed the concern of the doctor and nurses from the person to these implements. The film presents his reply to critics of his seemingly out-of-date practices: Schweitzer believed he knew of newer and advanced medical technologies, so much so that he could do without it, and make a practical mixture of old and new that suited his budget and his purposes.

The hospital compound, though bustling with activity, is marked throughout with Schweitzer's life project of atonement and his understanding of the brotherhood of those who bear the mark of pain. Reciprocity and empathy mark the acts of delivering others from pain, and this is the lesson of the hospital compound the viewer is to take from this film. The narrator recites Schweitzer's words of wanting us to become aware of the isolation one develops in daily life, and to not regard others as absolute strangers. The reserve we might feel in the presence of others is broken down, and so we should reach out to those others in hospitality, and thereupon become ourselves in doing so.

The final scenes of the film show Schweitzer retreating at the end of the day, to pursue his study and writing of philosophy, theology, and music in his small, cluttered room. The narrator earnestly utters that his work is never finished as there are "claims upon his heart." You do not hear Schweitzer himself talking much in the film aside from a scene where he greets people from his window in Günsbach. Otherwise, his words are spoken by the actor Fredric March, and the film is narrated by Burgess

Meredith. March's diction lends a solemnity to Schweitzer's written words, while Meredith's easily recognized voice brings a familiarity to American audiences, bridging the gap between the life of the typical viewer and the 50-year project of Schweitzer in Africa.

Le Grand Blanc de Lambaréné

In contrast, the recent African film *Le Grand Blanc de Lambaréné* is a critical and withering perspective on the work of the "great white doctor." Described in the *New York Times* online review as a "comedy,"[5] it is a revisionist view that takes liberty with the record. It is not the film's intent to portray Schweitzer with accuracy. The first scene is a brutal tooth extraction. The patient cries in pain as Schweitzer yanks the tooth out with pliers, with no anesthetic, the only comfort being a quick and almost uncaring douse of water. Schweitzer is portrayed as distant, vain, and egotistical, more intent upon his image and legacy than he is with those for whom he cares. His scholarly activities are scorned by the Africans, as we learn that they think he writes about Buddha at night because there is not enough to keep him busy during the day. Schweitzer's thought and writings to them are mostly all Western book learning, while he plays Western sacred music on his specially equipped piano. In a scene by the creek, the Africans claim that their science is not just writing, rather it is something alive, and relevant to their own lives.

A main character in the film is the African Kuomba. We first meet him as a boy, where he interacts with Schweitzer, and tells him he wants to be a doctor, presumably looking for a mentor. Schweitzer mockingly discourages Kuomba from this quest. Later in the film, Kuomba returns as the hope for African redemption and rebukes the influence of the great white doctor who dissuaded him from his dream as a young boy. Schweitzer is portrayed as similarly disinterested in the other Africans around him. He does not appreciate native customs. Even his relationship with his wife Hélène, almost mutely portrayed by the actress Marisa Berenson, is distant and cold, and he largely ignores her. Imperious and surly, he lectures the natives about venereal disease, and talks about Jesus as the savior.

Africa is dark and unknown to this Schweitzer, and the filmmaker makes this view vivid in Bissa, the African woman offered to him by a local chief, with whom Schweitzer dances and drinks wine. She says that he gives to the Africans, but does not share. This lack of cultural sharing is dramatized by the different music played by Schweitzer and the natives.[6] Late at night, Schweitzer attempts to drown out the African drumming outside his window with his piano-playing, calling the drummer a "tom tom maniac." Schweitzer is visited by a Western journalist, Ingrid Lombard, who takes mock-heroic photographs of him as he poses near the river. She later harshly criticizes his lifestyle, particularly the way he lives separately and eats different food, and he becomes angry at the dinner table, refuting her claims as she storms out of the dining room.

In the final part of the film, the Africans arise to overthrow Schweitzer and to celebrate their independence from colonial French rule. With pictures of Marx and Lenin on the wall, they talk of kicking him out of his hospital and having Kuomba run it. Independence in 1960 for Gabon is celebrated with music and festive activities, while Schweitzer is portrayed as bitter and forgotten, walking off in the distance. Kuomba, now a grown man, comes to him and says, "The independence of the people has never been your concern. You only wanted to share their hell in the hope of reaching your heaven."[7] For Kuomba and the other Africans, Schweitzer was so close to them for many years, but did not even bother to learn the language. It was a path that was open to him, and he of course knew many languages, but did not learn their language or customs to any degree, and thus did not experience their culture more directly. In this regard, his words scrolled on the screen at the film's end are ironic and unfulfilled: "All we can do is to allow others to discover us as we discover them."

Iconography

These two cinematic portraits of Schweitzer clash in intent, scope, and detail. They are different interpretations of the Schweitzer myth and legend. Another, more analytic and ordinary interpretation of Schweitzer resided in the public's consciousness from the time of his early work on the New Testament and Bach, increasing with the establishment of his hospital in 1913 and his own subsequent writings and the journalistic accounts of his work in Africa. He stood as a testament against the prevailing ethos of his age, which was materialistic, expansive, and self-regarding, but that is not what many people saw in Schweitzer. These people wanted an idol, someone to emulate. There are numerous accounts of people who uprooted their own lives to move to Lambaréné in order to work alongside him. As Montague notes there was the hero worshipper, the casual sightseer, the doubting Thomas, the gleaner, and the lunatic fringe.[8] All came to Lambaréné to see the white-haired "jungle doctor," some to work alongside him, if only for a brief time. This legend obstructs learning all that we can from his example. Schweitzer and his work still remain largely unknown at best or caricaturized at worst. Very few people know of Schweitzer's musical and scholarly accomplishments, while his work in Lambaréné usually brings forth these images, abetted by the two cinematic portrayals discussed, of the kindly if naïve elderly doctor among the natives or as a remnant of colonialism if it brings forth anything at all.

Schweitzer was celebrated when he was alive, but quickly became converted to an icon even before his death in 1965, thus becoming almost unapproachable. The legend that grew up around him was largely that of the selfless man, head shaded perpetually by a pith helmet, dispensing medical care to the native Africans, which makes the revisionist image in *Le Grand Blanc de Lambaréné* all the more thought-provoking and disturbing.[9] As with any legend, there is some truth, but it has been embellished. This image of Schweitzer serves as a convenient symbol of hero worship, but also is mainly true to the reality that he lived. However, that does not mean that we cannot examine what he did and learn from it, to rethink Schweitzer for our time, especially for education.[10]

There are a number of figures who chose such the path of "courage of conviction." Socrates comes to mind, as well as Augustine and Thomas More. Socrates lived with the conviction that he was to be the "gadfly" in the Athenian marketplace, rooted in this culture so much so that he refused exile. Augustine sought out this same rootedness in a community of believers, moving away from the profligacy of his earlier life to a committed Christianity. Thomas More lived out his life with resolution unto death famously portrayed in the play and film *A Man for All Seasons*.

Why, though, has Schweitzer moved to the background of discussion about philosophy and religion in our cultural life? Why has his work not been linked more directly to a theory and practice of education? In education, there has been a broad, though not deep, recognition of the work of Schweitzer. There are numerous Schweitzer schools around the world, either merely bearing his name or being inspired by his example. These schools vary in mission and curriculum. The fact that there have been so few systematic discussions of Schweitzer and education until now shows that his influence has not been linked to educational theory and practice.

I believe there are a number of reasons for this phenomenon of cultural and, specifically, educational neglect. These reasons include Schweitzer's solitariness, his particular form of Christianity and its connection to other religious traditions and forms of spirituality, and perhaps most importantly, his relationship to colonialism.

The Solitary Figure

Albert Schweitzer joined a missionary group in the Congo, but few chose to or could follow him on the difficult path he took. While he continued to write and play music, his work as a jungle doctor took him out of the mainstream, taking him on a unique journey for a European intellectual and accomplished author that many admired from afar. Schweitzer's level of commitment and the particularity of his unswerving faith make it hard to build a concerted effort or movement around his example. Though Schweitzer did allow others to learn about him and his work, like Socrates, he eschewed followers. That is the import of seeing the hospital at Lambaréné as an "improvisation" and his dictum of Reverence for Life as his most important contribution. There are many Lambarénés, and to not find them elsewhere but to insist upon that one project as privileged makes his work in Gabon a precious artifact, rather than a living example. Our moral imagination should be wider, Schweitzer seems to be saying, to send us into ourselves so that we may discover our own Lambarénés.

Christianity

Schweitzer was the son of a pastor and a committed Christian his entire life. His Christian faith forms the basis for his investigations into Jesus's life, and his work on the history of scholarship about Jesus. Schweitzer continued to serve as a minister to those at his hospital. In today's religious, social, and political climate, such a commitment can be easily misinterpreted. We see examples of devout Christians closing their minds to social change, such as the desire for full recognition as equals by women, gays, lesbians, and ethnic and racial minorities. Christian fundamentalists decry practices such as same sex marriage and abortion. Such practices are widespread, and even tolerated by the majority of people in many countries. On the other hand, a virulent brand of Islam betrays that religion's roots and long-established practices by envisioning an uncompromising war against the West, in particular, the open, democratic social practices that grant full rights to women, gays and lesbians, and other minorities.

There are significant criticisms of religion, many borne of a frustration with such socially conservative or fundamentalist practices. Perhaps just as important, many of us are distressed by the aversion to science and reasoning that seemingly accompanies certain religious worldviews. However, Schweitzer was a model of someone deeply knowledgeable about religion, philosophy, and the sciences. He himself was a practical scientist, in that he learned about medicine and other applied sciences, such as agriculture, and used them in his work at Lambaréné every day.

Colonialism

Discussing Schweitzer in the context of colonialism is complicated. He was drawn to Africa for reasons that can be generously said to be influenced by his culture and background. He heard of the dire conditions there and believed he was called to help. Schweitzer's own colonialism was part of his time, where he looked upon his mission in Africa in paternalistic terms, but he also criticized the rapaciousness of the colonial practices of logging and resource exploitation. Mike W. Martin points out the complexity of passing judgment on Schweitzer's work:

> For some observers, Schweitzer's mission of mercy becomes a tragic symbol of colonial oppression. Does Schweitzer's participation in colonialism undermine his ethical theory? That would be like saying Thomas Jefferson's participation in slavery undermines his theory of human rights. Both thinkers had large moral blind spots in applying their ethical theories, but that is no basis for rejecting the theories in entirety.[11]

Martin goes on to cite some of Schweitzer's pronouncements regarding Africa, in tune with a colonialist and paternalist viewpoint, but states that Schweitzer was anomalous to the more pronounced colonialism of the time.

Schweitzer was famously inspired by the melancholy "Negro" statue in Colmar to help those in need in the "dark continent." There are of course varying explanations and various levels of thinking about colonialism. We can look at the expression of spent and tired European cultural practices. Many intellectuals, artists, and social activists believed European civilization had become exhausted and was in need of revival. Schweitzer captured this in his "*Wir epigones*" dictum, that all that had come before was greater, and he and his European intellectuals at the time were mere "inheritors of the past." Schweitzer believed that through an active rather than contemplative life he would overcome this cultural exhaustion and *ennui*, and decided to do this by working as a physician in Africa. He notes how he was pleased to be sent to French Africa and was not allowed to preach. Thus he could work with his hands and make a direct contribution where it was needed most.[12] Schweitzer, for all his accomplishments as a scholar in Europe, did not see scholarship or even performing music as the avenue for his life's work. He wanted to do more through direct service to people he believed were in the greatest need.

Further insight into his conviction that such direct action aimed toward helping others is morally superior to preaching or scholarship is evident in accounts of how he interacted with people in Africa. The sources of documentation for this are the observations made by visitors, those who worked with him at Lambaréné, and his own writings. Schweitzer has been criticized by some who believe that he treated the African natives with colonial disregard. What Schweitzer did and did not learn from his work over the years with the Africans bears upon what we can take away for a Schweitzerian educational theory and practice. Robert Payne gives a more nuanced view of Schweitzer's relationship to colonialism:

> He was at once the slave of Lambaréné and its patriarch. He loved Lambaréné with a desperate and overwhelming love, but he remained a stranger there. As the years went by, he complained increasingly about the difficulty of knowing the natives; they lived in realms beyond his reach; only when they were mortally ill could he penetrate at intervals into the strange world they inhabited, illuminated by the lightning-gleams of primitive cults and a fierce fetish-worship. He was no anthropologist, and took little interest in their customs. Always he held himself a little in reserve.[13]

Payne seems to attribute some of Schweitzer's isolation from the natives to his advancing age, but also to the fact that Schweitzer was not as well-equipped as some to understand the customs and practices of the native people. He saw his work in Africa through his own lenses—a Christian and Jainist devotion borne of reflection and of penitent labor in helping others who are suffering.

Finally, the idea of colonialism is linked with how Schweitzer conducted medical practice at his hospital. In contrast to the critics of Schweitzer's hospital who focused upon the less-than-optimal hygiene and currency of medical practice, another side of Schweitzer's hospital is central to his educational legacy. The hospital in Lambaréné grew organically from the needs of the people and the situation in equatorial Africa. It stands as a material testament to how he viewed his experience in Africa. It is hard to see such a venture, still in operation and indeed thriving today, as merely an "improvisation," Schweitzer's term for his nearly half century of work in Africa, against what he saw as his main accomplishment, bringing the idea of Reverence for Life to understanding and practice. But by at least entertaining that idea of improvisation, we can see how Schweitzer remained open to certain practices that would not be considered by, say, a team of physicians bringing their medical science and technology *to* the jungle and applying more whole-scale external practices and ideas of caring for the sick. Schweitzer may not have been an anthropologist, nor did he learn the languages or customs of the people with whom he lived and worked for so many years. Yet, he did recognize the primacy of custom and of family in his medical ministrations.

Prophet and Paradigm

Schweitzer's influence upon education is in another indirect but powerful way, and that is as an *educational prophet*. Schweitzer's value may not be in any curriculum that he possibly could have proposed, but in his example to us of moving us to a vision of what might be in our educational lives.[14] The value of an educational prophet is in awakening others to what might be, and to warn others of the paths down which we are traveling.

If Schweitzer did not take the time to learn native languages nor practice the most modern hygienic and medical practices, one could see him as insensitive, or as Robert Payne did, as ruthlessly focused upon his own personal salvation and through it that of others: "*His mission was nothing less than to revive by his writing and by his example the lost purposes of western civilization.*"[15] Joseph Conrad saw in the heart of darkness what was screaming all around us, but Schweitzer called it forth. He was at heart a teacher, someone who called out, as William Ayers claims, the fundamental message of all teachers, that you can change your life.[16] The way that Schweitzer called this message forth was by his example and indeed his prophecy. As Jim Garrison and Roger Jones state in discussing a book on prophetic teaching, "Indeed, part of prophecy is to name the needed ideals in destitute times."[17] Bringing attention to these ideals that will help us revive lost or neglected purposes in education is part of Schweitzer's educational legacy.

David Purpel looks deeply into the prophetic tradition to develop a new "professional mythos" principally for educators that can "remind us of our highest aspirations, of our failure to meet these, and of the consequences of our responses to these situations."[18] If we take the uncompromising aspects of Schweitzer's work (his commitment to work in the difficult climate and living situation and his authoritarian demands that the hospital be a certain way), we can contrast this to what Purpel sees as the appeasement and passivity of today's educators with the Biblical prophets.[19] Schweitzer did this in action, rather than merely words. It is a calling forth, but the passion is directed toward caring and compassionate deeds in an imperfect world.

He is not a prophet in the sense that Abraham Joshua Heschel, cited by Purpel, sees:

> The prophet seldom tells a story, but casts events. He rarely sings, but castigates. . . . His images must not shine, they must burn. The prophet is intent on intensifying responsibility, is impatient of excuse, contemptuous of pretense and self-pity. His tone, rarely sweet or caressing, is frequently consoling and disburdening: his words are often slashing, even horrid-designed to shock rather than to edify. . . . [The Prophet is concerned with] wrenching one's conscience from the state of suspended animation.[20]

The Biblical prophet that Heschel and Purpel describe is an angry and insistent *vox clamantis in deserto* standing in sharp contrast to how Purpel describes teachers, as compliant and docile, dutifully carrying out the traditional and subservient "intellectual *gofer*" role of cultural transmission. Schweitzer was demanding and could be imperious and ruthless in his quest for not only his own personal renewal, but also societal transformation. He is a prophet as teacher described thus by Jim Garrison in his book on Dewey, where a teacher looks to create "alternative possibilities . . . if those possibilities turn out, on appraisal, to be truly desirable . . . to . . . imagine intensely beyond knowledge of established fact or any actual state of affairs."[21] This prophetic voice tempers its anger and channels it into deeds, calling out to others to find your own Lambaréné, as a hospital on the banks of the Ogooué River is but an "improvisation" as Schweitzer called it.

Schweitzer's educational prophecy calls us to do more in our teaching and learning in today's schools, to change our lives and those of others with whom we come in contact. Beyond the categorization of prophet, there is a related typology, lesser known and more exclusive. The German philosopher Karl Jaspers put forth the notion of a *paradigmatic individual*[22] in his philosophy of existence. He provides a concise but illuminating account of the thought and lives of unique leaders who came at the start of many of the great spiritual and philosophic traditions of the world. These men all took as part of their mission the guidance of the human spirit toward more basic and ultimate values, and they continue to influence the world today. There has been a concern about Jaspers's selection of these four individuals, begging the questions, "Why *these* men? Why only *four*? Why just *men*?" In presenting the lives and work of Socrates, Buddha, Confucius, and Jesus, the standard for Jaspers is ultimate:

> The four paradigmatic individuals have exerted a historical influence of incomparable scope and depth. Other men of great stature may have

been equally important for smaller groups. But when it comes to broad, enduring influence over many hundreds of years, they are so far above all others that they must be singled out if we are to form a clear view of the world's history.[23]

Jaspers goes on to both differentiate these figures as well as seek common ground. He considers other figures, including Old Testament prophets, as well as Mohammed, whom he considers historically important, but not with the individual depth of these four.[24] While arguments can be made about Jaspers's inclusiveness, it is more interesting to investigate his reasoning for the standard, and what we can learn to help us position Schweitzer and his accomplishments.[25]

The four paradigmatic figures of Jaspers's typology all had extraordinary impact, though none of them wrote anything nor did they seek followers. This did not matter for Jaspers, as their essence lay elsewhere, in their transformative power.

> The demands they make on us are never fully expressed in instructions that need merely be followed. In order to understand them, one must experience some sort of transformation, a rebirth, a new awareness of reality, an illumination.[26]

Each of the four paradigmatic individuals was unique. We look to each as the start of something, whether it is the rational inspection and inquiry of the soul with Socrates, or Buddha's contemplation and freedom from the cares of the world as a means toward salvation. Schweitzer saw that his hospital at Lambaréné, far from being his crowning achievement, was merely an example that others could learn from but not imitate. He believed his key accomplishment was the insight into Reverence for Life. That is why it was important to find one's own Lambaréné, and to pay heed to Reverence for Life rather than any particular work that was done by him to be followed or, worse, imitated. Jaspers writes:

> We become aware that in our own reality we follow none of them. Once the distance between our own questionable lives and the earnestness of these great men is brought home to us, we feel impelled to summon up all the earnestness of which we are capable. Herein they are beacons by which to gain an orientation, not models to imitate.[27]

Schweitzer's legacy for education is partly that of a beacon for orientation, and an imitative model. True to Schweitzer's own view, the beacon is more powerful and lasting, and that is what Schweitzer wanted for others, why

Lambaréné was for him improvisatory even as it has continued as a hospital today, and why those who came merely to be with him were sometimes disappointed. The imitative models of the Schweitzerian icon and myth industry are but pale copies, what Dewey called reduplications. These models are not alive and vital in the sense that they develop their own particular angle upon the legacy of Schweitzer. In considering this legacy, we educators are led to ask for our own time, of our own educational inventions and initiatives, by paraphrasing Schweitzer: Is the school the way?

9

Conclusion: Is the School the Way?

After Schweitzer had completed his major writings and was deep into his work at Lambaréné, Oskar Kraus wrote a brief assessment of him as a thinker. In the foreword to the first edition, Kraus goes to the heart of the intellectual appreciation of Schweitzer: While many have rejected his speculative ethics of Reverence for Life, his life's example and practical ethics have had the most impact.[1] Making his life his argument speaks to us from the particular time that Schweitzer lived, and transcends circumstance to make him still a potent spiritual force in the world and especially in education. Kraus wrote:

> I do not think I exaggerate when I maintain that the cultural world of today has produced no one who could equal Schweitzer in originality, in many sidedness, and in the intensity of his intellectual, his artistic, and above all his ethical qualities.[2]

We are fortunate in that we get Schweitzer's own words on the motivation for his life's work, from stepping out of being just a professor to acting and doing in the world in the first lines of his book *On the Edge of the Primeval Forest*: "I gave up my position of professor at the University of Strasbourg, my literary work, and my organ-playing, in order to go as a doctor to Equatorial Africa. How did that come about?"[3] He went beyond just the consideration of a possible need to actually enacting this work in an obstacle-ridden environment.

Few of us make this step toward such action. Yet, to teach demands a commitment that may not approach this level but that is certainly ridden with obstacles. Schweitzer continues with a discussion of the parable of

Lazarus and Dives, and applies it to society as a whole, not just to individuals. While his language is dated, the ideas are not.

> I had read about the physical miseries of the natives in the virgin forests; I had heard about them from missionaries, and the more I thought about it the stranger it seemed to me that we Europeans trouble ourselves so little about the great humanitarian task which offers itself to us in far-off lands. The parable of Dives and Lazarus seemed to me to have been spoken directly to us! We are Dives, for, through the advances of medical science, we now know a great deal about disease and pain, and have innumerable means of fighting them: yet we take as a matter of course the incalculable advantages which this new wealth gives us! Out there in the colonies, however, sits wretched Lazarus, the coloured folk, who suffers from illness and pain just as much as we do, nay, much more, and has absolutely no means of fighting them. And just as Dives sinned against the poor man at his gate because for want of thought he never put himself in his place and let his heart and conscience tell him what he ought to do, so do we sin against the poor man at our gate.[4]

There are a number of responses one could take in a similar situation, from concern to giving funds to actually committing oneself to help. Schweitzer shows recognition of the issue or problem, followed by empathy and sympathy, and then action. He goes further than almost every person in finding a way through medicine that demands even greater sacrifice.[5]

Spiritual and Cultural Regeneration

I have discussed the elements of his intellectual heritage in his biography that informed this decision, and set the context for his cultural and educational contributions. Schweitzer believed that he was living in a time of cultural decay, complete with a market-oriented life and an eroding of human relationships. This is not original, of course, for one only has to think of the American transcendentalists Ralph Waldo Emerson and Henry David Thoreau, as well as Spengler and Nietzsche, right up to poets such as Rainer Maria Rilke, who lyrically decried our age of manufactured over handmade objects. Obviously, too, this theme continues forward with Martin Heidegger's own particular brand of domesticity and with various environmental, living-small, and green movements today. Along with the dominance of markets in modern times come the twin burdens of nationalism and imperialism. Schweitzer lived through two world wars, suffering sickness as a prisoner of war in the first. He saw this world as being too small and limited, and the people in it too devoted to their own profit and gain. In his lifetime he witnessed an enormous growth in the natural sciences and technical fields, such that medical science eradicated or controlled many previously virulent diseases. Yet, Schweitzer repeatedly asks us to consider some of the most fundamental questions of life, and how we treat each and every person, and indeed, all living things.

Performativity and Accountability

Further erosion of the social and educational fabric has occurred since Schweitzer's time. Artists give us a portrait of this depletion. In Don DeLillo's novel *White Noise*,[6] Jack Gladney, the professor of Hitler Studies who speaks no German, faces a continuous barrage of health and safety warnings from such sources as the news media and the packaging on consumer goods. Jack feels a persistent dread and is obsessed with his own death. An endless stream of white noise, both technological and human, characterizes Jack's life. As he wades through the never-ending currents of data and chatter, this distraction, at once elusive and powerful, forms the basis for his life.

This dread for many people is not a primal fear, but as for the characters in Delillo's novel, a second order fear, diffuse and without an identifiable source, and similar to the fear and dread exploited by terrorists in their most extreme and manipulative stage. Terrorism plays upon the fear of a seemingly random act, a bus exploding, a hotel lobby shattering, or a jet piercing a building. But we also see, in subtler and perhaps more insidious form, this dread from all those seemingly helpful labels on consumer packages, warnings we get in popular media, and so forth. The world is not a safe place, no matter what our hyper-rationalized attempts at understanding, controlling, and even dominating our world have attempted to do.

One reaction to this is a hyper domesticity, signaled by our gated communities, our turning inward toward safe and constant items in our personal ecologies, such as companion animals, and our suspicion of strangers. We are surrounded by the advice-culture regime telling us how to raise and educate our children. The white noise of educational reform, replete with governmentality and performativity, suggests how our schools should be, what the role of students should be, but also, importantly, how parents should act. But we may fool ourselves if we see debates about educational reform and the raising of children as more than this performativity. Behind it lies, as Gene Glass notes, discussions that are "not about achievement or test scores or preparing tomorrow's workforce at all. They are about gaining the political power to control money and secure special privileges. Behind the rhetoric lies material self-interest, a drive for comfort, and a need for security."[7] In North America, Europe, and in the developed countries of Asia, we see this performativity pervading child-rearing standards and measures of educational accountability.

The modern age of educational reform began in the United States with the report *A Nation at Risk*, which alarmed America at the dawn of Ronald Reagan's presidency. As Berliner and Biddle point out in *The Manufactured Crisis*,[8] there was no evidence provided within that document, nor was evidence available, of a "rising tide of mediocrity" to the extent stated by the government. We looked to Japanese education as the model for what we needed to do, much as the reformers of the nineteenth century looked to Prussia. What the Japanese did could be imported into our thinking, colonizing it, because, quite frankly, Pacific Rim industrial output was beginning to rise and Japan finally made automobiles that were competitive in the American and European markets. What Berliner and Biddle found in studying the supposed educational crisis proclaimed by many reformers was a misuse and simplification of evidence to make the point about schools. So-called accountability in education is, of course, modeled on what passes for accountability in corporate America, namely productivity increases. The focus then becomes the school, the teacher, the building-level administrator, as simple industrial "inputs" as Frederick Taylor saw elements of factory production. This focus does not take into account the broader view of the cultural context of schooling, and the many social, economic, and political factors that go into making our schools what they are. Thus our schools become what Berliner calls, in a later book with Sharon Nichols,[9] an arena for "collateral damage." Nichols and Berliner show how high-stakes accountability, so prevalent in education today, is subject to Campbell's law: The more any quantitative social indicator is used for social decision-making, the more it will be subject to corruption pressures and the more apt it will be to distort and corrupt the social processes it was intended to monitor. We have seen in the United States how the performative accountability measures of the No Child Left Behind Act alter and subvert the curriculum and any other sort of assessment that does not lead straight to the performance standards so specified.

The dread and anxiety of our age may be generalized and free floating, but the reaction we have to it is insistent, technical, and precise.

We institute measures, rather than discuss widely what to do and then develop thoughtful ways of assessing what we needs to be assessed. We scapegoat others: It must be the fault of poor parenting, or low birth weight, or whatever. Such a hyper rational means/end instrumentality also crowds out more ancient, familial, and local lore, such as some of the research of my Diné (Navajo) graduate students to describe and elucidate indigenous ways of knowing that foreground custom, habit, and tradition.

Increasingly, we see schools as part of the market and the performative adult world rather than as a place to learn and to just *be*. The parent is a customer, and the customer seeks quality in a product. These market considerations link to school choice, where before schooling was bound by accident of place and residence, and it was the task of those leading and teaching in schools to create a community in the school as well as respond to the needs of the residents of that area and the children they sent to that school. Thus the bonds of schools in communities continue to be submerged and even lost. Parental involvement cannot be expected in ways other than to demand positionality for one's child and to get out of the relationship what one can, or more if you can swing it.

There is no feeding forward of a rich, multifaceted social culture that will nourish a *polis*. Instead customers want value, and at the same time, there is great government paternalism. Even though there is no accepted or settled concept of the good or how to raise children, there are technical experts who advise on health, creating the white noise of caution and cheery bromides aimed at creating and assuring positionality and relative advantage. Instead of a reciprocal understanding and mutual development of ways of upbringing and education for all children, we get "responsibilization" and a worry about making sure others know what to do. In the nineteenth century, such attitudes and practices were largely classist in my country with the advent of charity kindergartens for impoverished children, where hygiene was didactically taught and "Americanization" rooms were used to socialize these immigrants. Positionality reigns now, and thus the emphasis is upon the competition necessary to get kids into the best schools, rather than working to make better that school where one sends one's children.

Accountability and performativity are now joined with "safeguarding," as we would do with our "investments," in a time of dislocation and rapid change. Given the constraints upon government action, do we remake government into something that can abet achievement, equality, and protection for our children? Is this possible? What do we do about the way things have become? Are there other ways we can work together, in solidarity, to take back and at least be conscious of how we are raising our children and what role they should play? Must we always do and not just be, or must being be only reserved for times apart from school and learning? We humans are not congeries of instrumentalities. Parenthood is not a task to be checked off and completed. That is "parenting" with all its technical connotations. Parenthood, rather, is a mode of being. As such, we deprive ourselves of a fuller range of human experience when we look upon parenthood as simply parenting, as skills to polish a product, rather than a wider sense of being with, being alongside, or just being and perhaps just doing nothing in the presence of children. How far that is from our instrumentalism to create tomorrow's workforce in the current "upbringing industry" and in our schools.

Schweitzer's Response: Reverence for Life

Likewise, Schweitzer too was fully aware of a number of shifts in the locus of control for human life, from the human to the technological, the individual to the state, and Nature to industry.[10] In the first two of these modes, the more immediate is given over to that which is larger, and individual conscience and action are at least susceptible to subjugation. In the third, Nature has given way to industry, where again, subjugation is the mode of operation, rather than coexistence. For Schweitzer, the way out of these developments, at least in part, is to have Reverence for Life. A typical day at Lambaréné can show how inner motivation connects to outward action. This provides a different, privileged view of the work that is free from the two dominant portraits of the Schweitzer legacy, that of hagiographic representations and hero worship on one side, and damning depictions of filth, subjugation, and meager medical competence on the other.

Individual responsibility is paramount as one goes about using one's own life to make a statement, not only to oneself, but to others, and if so inclined as Schweitzer, as testament to one's religious faith. Schweitzer's emphasis upon service and enacting what one believes bears similarity to Johann Heinrich Pestalozzi's educational aim of the development of the whole person—not merely intellectual growth, but what Pestalozzi calls the hand, heart, and head. Here Pestalozzi is quoted by a biographer:

> I wish to wrest education from the outworn order of doddering old teaching hacks as well as from the new-fangled order of cheap, artificial teaching

tricks, and entrust it to the eternal powers of nature herself, to the light which God has kindled and kept alive in the hearts of fathers and mothers, to the interest of parents who desire their children grow up in favour with God and with men.[11]

Pestalozzi goes beyond Rousseau's view of individual, unencumbered learning to set out concrete ways based upon research. He reconciled the tension, recognized by Rousseau, between the education of the individual (for freedom) and that of the citizen (for responsibility and use). Schweitzer's own work at his hospital and the surrounding villages is part of this tradition. It is an environmental education based on an appreciation of the natural world but also our place within that world. We are to educate so that we understand that no person has the right to receive only benefits from nature and society, but that each has a responsibility to give back some part of ourselves to serve the greater good of the natural environment and the community of human beings. Schweitzer's work has lived on in schools today, but as we shall see, the legacy is not as strong as it could be.

Schweitzer in the Schools

There are a number of ways that Schweitzer's influence is evident in schools, from the simple naming of a school for him to a curriculum that has in varying degrees elements of Schweitzer's views. Schweitzer-inspired curricular projects include those conducted in the 1990s by centers that no longer exist, such as the Albert Schweitzer Center in Great Barrington, MA, and the Albert Schweitzer Institute for the Humanities at Choate Rosemary Hall School in Wallingford, CT. These projects in turn inspired ongoing curricular development at the Harmony Institute in Harmony, FL.

The components of these curricula include prefatory text about Schweitzer's life and views on education, such as the quote on the cover of *An Albert Schweitzer Activity Book: Curriculum Guide for Grades 1–6* produced in 1992 by the Albert Schweitzer Center in Massachusetts:

The school will be the way! From the time they start school, young people must be imbued with the idea of reverence for all living things. Then we will be able to develop a spirit based on ethical responsibility and one that will stir many. Then we will be entitled to call ourselves a humanity of culture.[12]

The guide includes activities a teacher can conduct to help students understand the life and work of Schweitzer, but the bulk of the guide is various hands-on activities divided into three additional sections: World Peace and Understanding; World Health; and The Environment and Animals. Under World Peace and Understanding, lessons include a peace ritual based on the incident where Schweitzer heard the church bells while on the hunt for the bird with the slingshot discussed earlier. The activities range from those that encourage awareness of others, to hands-on instruction on "oral hydration therapy," that points out how children in Mumbai, India, have learned the technique to prevent dehydration due to fever or diarrhea.

Another effort, the Albert Schweitzer Inter-School Service Project, was one of the major initiatives in the 1990s of the Albert Schweitzer Institute in Connecticut. It was conceived as a way to not only expose students to the work of Schweitzer, but to involve them in a service project in Suriname in March 1997. Students from public high schools in Wallingford, CT, as well as the private preparatory school Choate Rosemary Hall brought supplies to children in Suriname and performed service activities while there. Pictures in the manual show students engaged in helping others there: planting pineapples with Amerindian villagers; repairing a swing at the House for Sexually Abused Children; and playing basketball and volleyball with boys at the Juvenile Detention Center.[13]

The teaching at the institute, though short lived, had an effect upon the students. Nikki Lindberg served as an administrator in the program from 1995 to 1999 and states what is a modest though subtle goal: "I think we are giving young people the opportunity to ask questions and to discover reverence for life through Albert Schweitzer, what he did, what he thought, what he wrote, and what he stood for. Their world will certainly be the better for it."[14] The genesis for the work of the Albert Schweitzer Institute where Lindberg worked came earlier, in a major conference at the United Nations in 1990 on the twenty-fifth anniversary of Schweitzer's death, that dealt with "subject areas of particular interest to Dr. Schweitzer: health, the environment, animal and human rights, theology, music, and world peace."[15] While these topics are familiar Schweitzer material, the transformation of their importance into an educational initiative is not equally represented in the work of Schweitzer, and that is what happened with the work of the institute. It took as its mission statement the following: "To perpetuate Albert Schweitzer's philosophy of reverence for life through programs of education and action."[16] Unfortunately, the institute was short lived, and perpetuation via its programs did not occur. The joining of two public high schools and an exclusive private preparatory school in this venture was notable, but the number of students affected, five each from the high schools as well as five from the prep school, was small. Still, the outcomes for individual students were profound and may even have been lasting.[17]

While the work in Connecticut may have been short lived institutionally, another program that grew out of the same roots encompasses not only classroom interaction, but the ecology of the school within a larger, intentional community that explicitly draws upon Schweitzer's writings and example. The community itself, because it is intentional and guided by these ideals, is a Schweitzerian educational practice. When the Harmony Institute was established in central Florida in 1996 and incorporated the next year, the founders envisioned an educational program informed by Albert Schweitzer's work a half century earlier. The institute was part of a planned community called Harmony, the second-largest private land development in Florida after the nearby Walt Disney World Resort. Four themes were interwoven in activities throughout each year in an early curricular iteration, called the "compassionate curriculum": respect for all that lives, caring for others, courage to act responsibly, and appreciation of differences. The students explicitly study the life and work of Albert Schweitzer in books titled *My Book about Albert Schweitzer, Albert Schweitzer: Humanitarian,* and *Albert Schweitzer: A Man for Our Times.* Later iterations of the curricular work at Harmony replaced the compassionate curriculum with a more directly interactive curriculum called the Youth "Living in Harmony with Nature" Education Program, where students and parents overtly focus upon Schweitzer's thoughts in conversations both at the school and at home.[18]

The Harmony Institute and the town of Harmony are governed by restrictions and covenants that interact with the curricular intent and offerings of the community. The planning of the community reflects Schweitzer's views about wise stewardship. The best way to see how the covenants and the curriculum inform each other is to examine them and compare their intent and focus. Two introductory sections of the covenant document are the relevant portions to examine. The first is the statement of general intent:

This document provides a framework for governing the interactions among humans, companion animals and wildlife in Harmony as well providing for the use and preservation of Harmony's natural and wildlife habitat areas. The overall goal of Harmony is to promote the peaceful coexistence of these human and animal residents within the community while striking a balance between the preservation, use and enjoyment of Harmony's natural areas.

Underlying these objectives are the values of fostering a respect for the land, the protection of wildlife and the sensible use and enjoyment of Harmony's abundant natural and manmade amenities by its residents. Animals are treasured members of the Harmony community. Promoting the bonds between people and all animals, safeguarding the welfare of animals within the community now and in the future, and serving as a model to other communities for the humane treatment of all animals are guiding principles of Harmony.[19]

These guiding principles set out how humans and animals should coexist in the community, but do not set out how these should be put into operation, which is done in the next section of the covenant, entitled "Harmony and Its Environment" that states particular educational aims and objectives:

Harmony incorporates natural and human-built environments that blend in ways designed to enhance the relationships between humans and animals and maximize the benefits of their peaceful coexistence. While retaining natural areas, Harmony is part of a human-dominated landscape where human actions profoundly affect the welfare of wild animals. This document seeks to articulate a philosophy that allows natural elements to persist unimpeded by humans and minimizes the circumstances that lead to conflict between humans and wildlife. Harmony's stewardship concept involves balancing hands-off and hands-on approaches.

These Rules do not anticipate all aspects of current and future relationships between humans and animals at Harmony that may need to be addressed. Therefore, these guiding principles and recommended approaches are intended to be dynamic and open-ended to allow the community to explore and adopt new and better conflict resolution strategies, landscape management schemes, environmental management techniques and practical approaches to maintaining biotic integrity. Harmony begins with a humane concept for its relationship with wild animals and continues to redefine that concept within the context of our larger society as well as in Harmony. An unchanging belief that wild animals deserve respect and should be free of human interference and allowed to interact with humans on their own terms will guide this evolving process.

In relation to wildlife and to the environment in which they live, the goals of the Harmony community are:

- To promote an understanding of how connected humans are to wildlife and to the surrounding environment.
- To foster tolerance, respect, and understanding of all living things.

- To provide opportunities for Harmony residents to view, hear, and interact with local flora and fauna in an ecologically and environmentally friendly way.
- To create and provide educational activities which will foster a community-wide land ethic and promote future land stewardship.[20]

To accomplish these ends in the community, a key factor is a curriculum in the schools that will foster understanding of the principles of the early planning captured in the covenant document. At first, the Harmony Institute developed its extensive "compassionate curriculum" in its charter school and in the public schools built on the property. This curriculum had two functions: "First, it supplements and enhances the standards-based curricula the students are already learning in math, reading, science, humanities, art, etc. with engaging activities. Second, it cultivates compassionate, active leadership; integrity; and informed, reasoned philanthropy."[21] Each grade level is characterized by a theme, skill focus, and developmental context. Thus, the skill focus for the first grade is to develop a "strong foundation for empathy," and the developmental context takes into account that children at this age value peers in addition to family members, and that an incipient moral sense of fairness is present in their dealings. The development of children as leaders is a tantalizing idea of the curriculum. Leadership here is not management, nor is it even really showing initiative. It is more a set of character traits that enable the children to realize they are part of a larger whole: "When we talk about leadership, we envision a young person who can work well with others—who knows when to talk and when to listen."[22] Modeling by both teachers and older students reinforced these moral and leadership lessons. However, the curriculum itself did not contain a sufficient number of concrete descriptions of activities, and it was never enacted in a systematic or complete sense in the schools at Harmony.

While the compassionate curriculum bore resemblances to other Schweitzer-inspired educational plans, it was more a sketch with a few iterations rather than a complete and extensive structure for teaching and learning. The impetus for the compassionate curriculum led to the development of a more robust plan now being carried out in the public schools in the town and surrounding county. This new and evolved curriculum connects the school, family, and community. The institute now works with families to develop an awareness of Schweitzer's philosophy and particularly the relation of humans in the natural world. This awareness is accomplished through "in-take questions" of the "Living in Harmony with Nature: A Partnership Program,"[23] posed to children to gauge their level of knowledge and awareness of their relationship to nature and their place in the natural world as they embark on the program. The questions range from asking if wild animals need a place of their own, to asking if it is important to try to kill bacteria and germs in one's home. With this basis for understanding the child's orientation toward the natural world and place within it, the curriculum attempts to build a connection to Schweitzer's work and beliefs. This understanding is mostly accomplished through reading and discussing the life of Schweitzer, particularly short quotes from his writings.

The curriculum seeks to help children learn about Schweitzer's philosophy, how to implement the principles of this philosophy in the planned community, and how to argue and advocate for these principles. Each discussion is guided by a quote from Schweitzer and there are questions to elucidate some of the meaning of Schweitzer's ideas. Perhaps more importantly, these sessions allow the children and their parents to engage in dialogue about a chosen text, and to relate it to their lives and how they will live in the community. It is a difficult task to make real and meaningful ideas beyond a curricular framework. The development of knowledge, implementation, argument, and advocacy are ambitious objectives, and research needs to be done to determine how effective these activities are.

Educational change and innovation are challenging to disseminate and replicate. A former colleague, visiting a new location for a beloved restaurant, paraphrased the late Seymour Sarason to "beware of new locations." Educational models of change interact with each other, from top-down mandates of national accountability and assessment standards such as the No Child Left Behind act in the United States, to local innovations proposed by a few teachers to meet a specific need. The problems for schools are that innovation is often imposed from outside the school walls by well-meaning though naïve policymakers. Thus, the landmark educational initiative called No Child Left Behind has the admirable goals to provide adequate education for all, but the means of accomplishing this emphasize high-stakes testing and summative accountability measures. Teachers experience what many researchers have confirmed, that there is a relationship between the emphasis upon such summative measures and the narrowing of the curriculum to meet the minimum standards of these measures. All else in the curriculum that does not get measured and assessed, or, just as likely, that is difficult to assess with simple and inexpensive tests, gets crowded out.

In spite of these challenges, I believe the meditation upon Schweitzer's words in the context of this modern planned community in central Florida can begin to point to an effective development of the character-building traits of knowledge, implementation, argument, and advocacy. In the penultimate session on Thursday, August 14, 2009, the students discussed this quote from Schweitzer:

> The friend of nature is the man who feels himself inwardly united with everything that lives in nature, who shares in the fate of all creatures, helps them when he can in their pain and need, and as far as possible avoids injuring or taking life.[24]

Students discussed the difficult questions of whether it might be necessary to take the life of a wild animal, just as Schweitzer had to make these life-and-death decisions at Lambaréné.[25] The questions enable the students to move from a knowledge of what the terms mean, to the implementation in the community, and finally toward those aspects of self-realization, being able to argue and to advocate for change or a way of life.

The influence of Schweitzer in primary and secondary education is limited for the most part to the naming of schools and these inchoate or recent curricular innovations. Schweitzer's influence in higher education is more pronounced, though perhaps no more innovative than initiatives done before college. The Albert Schweitzer College in Churwalden, Switzerland, was established in 1952 with summer courses and started a year-long course of study in 1955. Hans Casparis, who founded the college and served as director, developed his program model not only from the work and writings of Schweitzer, but also to some degree on the educational philosophy and practices of John Dewey.[26] More detailed discussions of how certain colleges and universities have attempted to incorporate Schweitzer are now available. In recent years, the Schweitzer Institutes at Quinnipiac University in Connecticut and Chapman University in California not only keep alive the memory of Schweitzer, but have run programs for college students and members of the community. Each institute has sponsored a conference that has resulted in a book[27] and each institute continues to offer classes and other activities.

The work at Chapman University is now led by Marvin Meyer, director of the institute there, and features a course, "Albert Schweitzer: His Life and Thought," taught annually in peace studies, philosophy, and religious studies.[28] Undergraduates "confront issues that may be addressed in the context of Schweitzer's ethic of reverence for life: finding meaning in life through twelve-step programs, making everyday decisions, setting standards for eating, deciding on abortion, considering the rights of animals, and living a life of responsibility in action"[29] and includes entries from students on these issues.

While this course at Chapman is typical for a liberal arts curriculum in its discussion and reading of texts, the insights that students brought to their reflections upon Schweitzer are unusual and come from a deeper place within them than that many undergraduates produce in commenting upon a course's required reading. Joie Karnes relates Schweitzer's resolve in his work in Africa to the twelve-step program of Alcoholics Anonymous:

> Alcoholics and addicts of all sorts are finding meaning in life in just the way Schweitzer prescribes. Through twelve-step programs people must accept their subordination to world events and develop inner freedom and serenity, and to keep life they are told they have to give it away in the service of others. The basic premise is that of reverence for life . . . Personal responsibility for all of a person's actions (which Schweitzer also emphasized) is crucial to twelve step programs and is also an essential component of reverence for life.[30]

Another student, Maria Tafoya, contemplates the inherent contradictions in the need to preserve a life (an organism such as an animal)—one may need to annihilate another organism (bacteria). She critically evaluates the Jain doctrine of ahimsā and sees that Reverence for Life includes an active component of changing the world for the better.[31]

Courses on Schweitzer also are part of the curriculum at Quinnipiac University, the home of another Schweitzer Institute. Students from nursing, physical therapy, occupational therapy, and the schools of Education and Law enact service projects in Nicaragua and Barbados, such as building additional classrooms for a school, planting vegetable gardens, and working in rural health clinics in Nicaragua, to providing training sessions in nursing, occupational, and physical therapy in Barbados.[32]

The work done at Chapman and Quinnipiac universities embeds Schweitzer in a traditional liberal arts curriculum, and has included components of what is called "service-learning." A less developed but ambitious curricular innovation inspired by Schweitzer began in 2004 with the planning of the Albert Schweitzer College in Minnesota. The innovator behind this venture is John Miller, the stepson of Rhena Schweitzer Miller. While the college itself has not been realized, Miller has developed a holistic approach to education that goes beyond a focus upon Reverence for Life to look to Schweitzer's life and multifaceted interests as an inspiration for a similar curriculum. Here Miller describes those interests and how the college planned to enact them:

- Intellect: Schweitzer was a theologian, philosopher, professor, and medical doctor.
- Creativity: Schweitzer was a world-class musician, and an expert on pipe-organ restoration.
- Environment: Schweitzer said, "I am life that wills to live, in the midst of life that wills to live," always considering the needs of the plants and animals—even the microbes—around him. His core ethic of Reverence for Life flashed upon him in a moment of transcendent communion with nature, while gazing at a herd of hippopotami in the Ogooué River at sunset.
- Service: Schweitzer acted locally, making the rounds each day at his hospital in Lambaréné, Gabon. He also exerted a global influence—first as a writer; then as a campaigner for peace, nuclear disarmament, and animal rights; and, ultimately, as a recipient of the Nobel Peace Prize.
- Self-Knowledge and Inner Development: Schweitzer was both a philosopher and theologian. His path of inquiry ranged widely, including studies of stoicism, Christianity, Jainism, Buddhism, and western philosophy (particularly that of Immanuel Kant). He strove to find a universal guiding ethic which could be fully explicable within a rational, non-religious framework (arrived at, he believed, in the understanding and practice of Reverence for Life).

Thus, the Schweitzer approach to education developed here will challenge students to engage in a correspondingly full range of activities. It will be holistic and integrated in that, alongside (a) academic learning, students will (b) engage in artistic and creative activities, (c) cultivate an experiential awareness of the natural environment, (d) engage in meaningful service, and (e) develop an individualized inner practice leading to increased self-knowledge and ethical action in the world.[33]

The framework that Miller proposes is similar to the knowledge, implementation, argument, and advocacy model of the Harmony Institute. Both carry out in varying degrees a practical reverence in an educational setting.

From Wish to Fulfillment

Schweitzer's Nobel Peace Prize speech supports a curriculum based on problems, rather than subjects, certainly a way of looking at schooling consonant with current curriculum theory. Schools that bear Schweitzer's name abound, as do institutes, centers, and initiatives. Educational theory without practice is hollow, and Schweitzer's influence has been examined in studies of curriculum.[34] However, what educational theory has taken from Schweitzer has not resulted in profound changes in educational practice beyond these limited and scattered examples. For the man who said he had schoolmaster's blood in him,[35] enactment of his legacy is partial and wishful. It is difficult to disseminate educational ideas and ideals and the slight influence of Schweitzer's work upon current schooling is ironic, given that he believed that "the school will be the way." While I do not doubt the sincerity of intention and purpose, the world of education turns a slightly deaf ear toward these efforts. I believe the reasons for this have to do with the Schweitzer myth and legend.

Toward the end of his life, Schweitzer became the target of withering criticism of his efforts in Lambaréné. His kindly and seemingly selflessly devoted image promoted throughout the world in the wake of his visit to the United States in 1949 and his subsequent Nobel Peace Prize a few years later raised him to the level of celebrity. Celebrity begets attention and, of course, those who doubt sincerity of purpose. Schweitzer was attacked for colonialist practices born of a nationalism that he himself despised. His hospital was roundly criticized for what many Western observers saw as backward practices and unsanitary conditions. These lingering images at the end of his life have contributed to what may be an eclipse of his influence, and a questioning of his legacy.

No human being is perfect, and it is certainly important to investigate the work of any person with an open mind. Yet, the characterization of Schweitzer as a tyrannical, racist, colonialist European absorbed by his own megalomaniacal needs that reached its apogee in the film *Le Grand Blanc de Lambaréné* is unwarranted. There are other perspectives, far more modest and even self-mocking. Werner Picht notes that

> in his old age Schweitzer contents himself with the thought that his ideas are now scratching around "like hens in the barnyard of world thought." And thus every "fellow warrior" in spirit is welcome, if only he helps spread these ideas.[36]

These ideas were his, but not his alone. They are to be considered by others with the gravity in which they were conceived, and his life as his argument can too be considered. Schweitzer did not intend to create an empire of his own thought.

Even if we were able to construct a vibrant educational theory and curriculum around at least some of his ideas, can we see Schweitzer as inspiration for us as we move forward in this already turbulent century?

What more can he give us as an example that can be useful in schools? We can look to his devoted life of service, and how he articulated a philosophy of ethical conduct, as partial guidance as we address environmental and global policy issues today. Rushworth Kidder, head of the Institute for Global Ethics, declares that we will not survive the new century using the ethics of the last. However, I believe that the ideas Schweitzer has articulated, and the life he led, can become at least part of a foundation for a new ethics, and can be enacted more forcefully and systematically in our schools. We can look to what Schweitzer says about all life being interconnected and interdependent as we make the argument that life itself must be held in reverential awe. It is this idea of reverence, as I have discussed in Schweitzer's case and developed into the idea of practical reverence that we can develop in our schools and social institutions. Individual responsibility is important, too, as one makes their life the argument for what they stand. Individual action is always important, even in an age of large organizations and bureaucratic emphases around the world. After all, it is only individual action for which each of us is completely responsible and that we can originate and control.

Schweitzer's intellectual and spiritual journey continues to influence many people in a number of fields. What contributes to that influence is certainly not his medical mission, as that is hardly unprecedented, and any number of people have done much the same. As important as his insights and his dictum of Reverence for Life are for many people, his ethical philosophy has not proven to be influential, and it is not well understood. Schweitzer's value lies in his ability to think his ideals through from foundation to practical application, and then to so fully live them.[37] His authority comes from what he has done, having made his life his argument, and he did more than just talk about what should be done sometime and by someone.

Is the School the Way?

I suggest here that one of Schweitzer's most profound legacies has not yet reached fruition, and there are many obstacles to it. That legacy, signaled by his statement "the school will be the way," is in educational thought, and more importantly, in the practices inspired by this thought in the lives of teachers and students in the schools of today and tomorrow. Reflection upon Schweitzer's resolve can serve easily enough to prompt further reflection upon what motivates each and every educator. He said that "one thing I know, the only ones among you who will be happy are those who will have sought and found out how to serve."[38] A teacher wants to move minds, and hearts, along to something better, more comprehensive, or more fulfilling. Teachers should be optimistic about what kind of effect they will have on their students. This effect should be transformative, even if the teacher only believes in the transmission and preservation of established knowledge. Otherwise why would one want to instruct the young?

Schweitzer's resolve shows how he came to join an inner examination to the outer action of his spiritual journey. He began this journey by reflecting upon his childhood experiences, such as the slingshot and the bird that had been a moment of moral revelation. He grew to become accomplished as a pastor, professor, and musician, but did not feel morally satisfied with these directions for his life. He exchanged letters with his future wife, Hélène Bresslau, over a long period of time before finally marrying and leaving Europe for Africa. The letters document his moral transformation, and often seem one-sided. Hélène Bresslau facilitates his moral development as she listens and responds to his thoughts and decisions on this quest. As they both embarked for Africa in 1913, he to stay there and work in difficult conditions for most of his remaining life without his wife, Schweitzer had completed the initial joining of his inner moral resolve to outer action. He drew upon his early life's moral lessons, the support of his absent wife and daughter, and many others to continue his work.

I discussed earlier the diary of the young Dutch woman Etty Hillesum that she kept during the Holocaust. David T. Hansen notes what is remarkable about the words she wrote in the midst of the chaos and social disintegration around her. Hillesum engaged in a moral and spiritual transformation of "harmonizing the inner and the outer."[39] The end result of this transformation is what Hansen calls "tenacious humility."[40] Such a state of mind and spirit is not static of course. One is tenacious over a long period of time, in the face of adversity, holding onto ideals in the face of doubt and difficulties. Hansen describes individuals in history and in literature who have this character trait, and it is worth citing his description at length.

> They attest to the struggles involved in overcoming self-interest, anger at the world, resentment or dislike of others, self-doubt, and more. They are tenacious in seeking meaning in life, which for them is another way of describing self improvement, but they are not always confident or optimistic about their quest for meaning. Nor are they always successful, in the external sense of that term; they do not always earn public notice or recognition.

Moreover, they are distressed and confused by the fact that they do not always have a good influence on others, their hopes notwithstanding. They are humbled by their limitations and by the natural and social constraints placed on their agency and on that of other people. They do not always overcome feelings of envy, avarice, pride, and impatience. In a nutshell, they provide language and images for common, but easy-to-forget, knowledge: that life is both trying and blessed, that dwelling with others is both very difficult and very necessary, and that moral ideals of personhood can help one find the way even when things grow dark.[41]

The first two sentences of Hansen's description capture Schweitzer throughout his life. He fought against self-regarding emotions as a young boy, through his early work as a pastor and preacher, displaying these emotions in a torrent of letters to his future wife, Hélène Bresslau. He overcame adversity in building, and rebuilding, his hospital in the jungle. Unlike the often unheralded men and women that Hansen describes, Schweitzer was well known in his endeavors from the time he was a young man and an accomplished scholar and musician who put this aside to serve others in a totally new profession, as a physician in the tropics far from the halls of learning and music in Europe.

At the opposite end of his life from his youth as a pastor, professor, and musician, he endured savage criticism at the same time that he became a celebrated figure and Nobel Prize winner. Many saw Schweitzer, at worst, as a fraud or evil colonialist, a patronizing European who imperiously imposed his will upon a developing African nation, who did not bother to learn the languages or much else about his surroundings during the 50 years he lived there. At best, as W. E. B. DuBois grants him, some saw Schweitzer as merely a doddering, misguided, and naïve figure, dwarfed by a larger world-historical set of changes on a vast continent, practicing out-dated medicine in a filthy and chaotic "hospital." But DuBois pauses in his approbation of Schweitzer and tempers it, seeing the power in his example of one person devoted to an ideal. Such an example, DuBois avers, can start a change in the world, even as it starts in a small and imperfect way.

Conscience in Action

We might imagine that Schweitzer would agree with this judgment by DuBois. He was called to do this work in Africa, and never intended the work itself to be the end result of his spiritual journey. Lambaréné was not meant to be an end result of a spiritual exploration and service to others. It is a small effort nonetheless, and one might even go so far with DuBois as calling it pitiful and insignificant in itself. But Schweitzer, a flawed human being like the rest of us, continued and persisted with his work. At the same time many of the worshipful Schweitzer disciples saw him as a paragon and attempted to emulate him or even just be alongside him. Others either laughed at what they considered naïve and meager achievements or damned what they considered patronizing colonialism.

After growing up in a close and traditional household as a young boy, Schweitzer was separated from his family when he attended Gymnasium. Homesick and diffident about his studies, his grades suffered and he risked losing his scholarship. One of Schweitzer's biographers, Herman Hagedorn, tells what happened next:

> Yet three months later he was in the upper group of his class. The miracle was performed quite unconsciously by a new teacher who did his own work with such precision that the boy could not bear to face what such a paragon must think of him, detached and slipshod as he was. His grades rose at a sharp angle. But, more important, he began to have a faint glimmer of what teaching meant. Not to stuff another's mind with facts, not even to train another's mind to think. *To present an example of conscience in action—that was teaching.*[42]

Schweitzer knew that teaching, like attending to tropical diseases and leprosy in a small hospital, may only be a singular act by one person, a small incremental gesture that may go unnoticed on the world's stage. However, we can be content to teach and learn alongside others, as Hansen's teachers do in their tenacious humility. We may sometimes fail to reach our students, but at other times, both we who teach and those who learn alongside us may have an epiphanic moment of discovery that illuminates a concept or a new field of endeavor, or just something about ourselves. At other times, we may feel lucky to gain knowledge or self-mastery in a hard win that demands time, energy, and sacrifice. In our work in educating the young while also educating ourselves, we teachers and other educators still may find the way when times grow dark. We may only be known to ourselves, pupils, friends, and even our god or gods if we wish, to paraphrase what Sir Thomas More says to Richard Rich in *A Man for All Seasons*.[43] And in this endeavor, we have Albert Schweitzer alongside us:

> Of all the will toward the ideal in mankind only a small part can manifest itself in public action. All the rest of this force must be content with small and obscure deeds. The sum of these, however, is a thousand times stronger than the acts of those who receive wide public recognition. The latter, compared to the former, are like the foam on the waves of a deep ocean.[44]

Image 9.1   Schweitzer at Lambaréné

Back cover of *Finding Lambaréné*. Courtesy of Marvin W. Meyer. Photograph by Donald Desfor.

Notes

Preface

1. In addition to an unpublished doctoral dissertation, Ron Abrell's three published works on Schweitzer are "Albert Schweitzer: Educator for a Season," *Contemporary Education XLVI* (1) (1974): 28–33; "The School will be the Way," *Humane Education* (1978): 10–11; "The Educational Thought of Albert Schweitzer," *The Clearing House 54*(7) (1981): 293–96.
2. Alan M. Beck and Anthony G. Rud, Jr., "Kids and Critters in Class Together," *Phi Delta Kappan 82*(4) (2000): 313–15.
3. For a discussion of the theory and practice of teacher renewal at NCCAT, see Anthony G. Rud, Jr., and Walter P. Oldendorf, eds., *A Place for Teacher Renewal: Challenging the Intellect, Creating Educational Reform* (1992; repr., Charlotte, NC: Information Age Publishing, 2008).
4. The Quaker adage of "let your life speak" is adapted from the words of one of the founders of the Religious Society of Friends, George Fox: "Let your lives preach."

Chapter 1

1. These reflections by Schweitzer come when he is looking back on his youth as a man who is nearly 50 years old. Marvin Meyer notes the difficulty of understanding Schweitzer's own words: "When reflecting on his childhood, Schweitzer observed that the commandment not to kill and torture impacted him in a powerful way in his childhood and youth, and such may well be the case. It may well be that Schweitzer was predisposed from childhood and influenced by childhood experiences to feel a kinship with other living beings, a feeling that may anticipate his later affirmations of reverence for life. Yet Schweitzer's reflections, published in his *Memoirs of Childhood and Youth*, are based upon his sessions in 1923 with the psychologist and pastor Oscar Pfister in Zurich. . . I suggest that Schweitzer may in fact have projected his values as an ethical thinker in his mid-forties back upon the experiences of his childhood." Marvin Meyer, "Affirming Reverence for Life," in *Reverence for Life: The Ethics of Albert Schweitzer for the Twenty-First Century*, ed. Marvin

Meyer and Kurt Bergel (Syracuse, NY: Syracuse University Press, 2002), 24–25. Hereafter Meyer and Bergel, *Reverence for Life.*

2. James Brabazon starts his book with a portrait of this region, and calls Schweitzer "completely a man of Alsace." He continues by stating that "[O]ne can begin to understand him better if one begins by understanding this obstinate, friendly, self-reliant little region; a region that can never afford to ignore the march of history but refuses to be impressed by it, that lives close to the soil because the soil is good and profitable and is all that people have." James Brabazon, *Albert Schweitzer: A Biography*, second edition (Syracuse, NY: Syracuse University Press, 2000), 2. Hereafter Brabazon.

3. "Unitas Fratrum: The Moravian Unity of the World Wide Moravian Church. Origin and Growth of the Unitas Fratrum," http://www.unitasfratrum.org/pages/origin_and_growth.html.

4. Albert Schweitzer, *Essential Writings*. Selected with an Introduction by James Brabazon (Maryknoll, NY: Orbis, 2005), 13. Hereafter *EW*.

5. Albert Schweitzer, *Memoirs of Childhood and Youth*, trans. Kurt Bergel and Alice R. Bergel (Syracuse, NY: Syracuse University Press, 1997), 39. Hereafter *Memoirs.*

6. Ibid., 37.

7. There is a growing literature on this topic. See Mark R. Dadds, "Conduct Problems and Cruelty to Animals in Children: What is the Link?" in *The International Handbook of Animal Abuse and Cruelty: Theory, Research, and Application,* ed. Frank R. Ascione (West Lafayette, IN: Purdue University Press, 2008), 111–128.

8. *Memoirs,* 39.

9. See the discussion of motivations for cruelty to animals in Dadds, "Conduct Problems and Cruelty to Animals in Children," 116.

10. Jerome Hill and Erica Anderson, *Albert Schweitzer* (Troma Entertainment, 2005.) (Original film produced in 1957). Hereafter Hill and Anderson.

11. *Memoirs,* 38–39.

12. Ibid., 41.

13. Marc Bekoff proposes that animals do in fact exhibit moral behavior, which is not simply humans anthropomorphizing what animals do. See, in particular, Marc Bekoff, *The Emotional Lives of Animals: A Leading Scientist Explores Animal Joy, Sorrow, and Empathy—and Why They Matter* (Novato, CA: New World Library, 2007); and Marc Bekoff and Jessica Pierce, *Wild Justice: The Moral Lives of Animals* (Chicago: University of Chicago Press, 2009).

14. *EW*, 164–165.

15. *Memoirs,* 49–50.

16. Ibid., 50.

17. Ibid., 53

18. Brabazon, 75–76.

19. *Memoirs,* 57–58.

20. Ibid., 64–65.

21. Ibid., 66–67.

22. Ibid., 78.

Chapter 2

1. Albert Schweitzer, from "Die Philosophie und die allgemeine Bildung im neunzehnten Jahrhundert," 68, trans. Charles R. Joy, in *Albert Schweitzer: An Anthology*, ed. Charles R. Joy (Boston: Beacon, 1967), 305. I thank Jack Fenner for bringing this quotation to my attention.

2. James Brabazon, *Albert Schweitzer: A Biography*, second edition (Syracuse, NY: Syracuse University Press, 2000), 68. Hereafter Brabazon.

3. Kant wrote three "critiques," of pure reason, practical reason, and aesthetic judgment. The categorical imperative of Kant's critique of practical reason, like the dictum of Reverence for Life, is an intuitive insight into the core of one's moral being and guides action in the world.

4. Charles R. Joy, "Introduction," in Albert Schweitzer, *Goethe: Five Studies*, trans. Charles R. Joy (Boston: Beacon, 1961), 3. Hereafter, *Goethe: Five Studies*.

5. Brabazon, 75.

6. Albert Schweitzer, "The One Hundredth Anniversary Memorial Address," in *Goethe: Five Studies*, 85.

7. *Goethe: Five Studies*, 4.

8. Albert Schweitzer, "The One Hundredth Anniversary Memorial Address," 88–89.

9. Ibid., 81.

10. Ibid., 82.

11. *Goethe: Five Studies*, 16–17.

12. Ibid., 18.

13. Albert Schweitzer, "Goethe the Philosopher," in *Goethe: Five Studies*, 123.

14. Mark E. Jonas, "A(R)evaluation of Nietzsche's Anti-democratic Pedagogy: The Overman, Perspectivism, and Self-Overcoming," *Studies in Philosophy and Education, 28*: 159.

15. Ibid., 164.

16. Ibid., 166.

17. Marvin Meyer, "Affirming Reverence for Life," in *Reverence for Life: The Ethics of Albert Schweitzer for the Twenty-First Century*, ed. Marvin Meyer and Kurt Bergel (Syracuse, NY: Syracuse University Press, 2002), 28.

18. Jackson Lee Ice, *Albert Schweitzer: Sketches for a Portrait* (Lanham, MD: University Press of America, 1994), 24. Hereafter Ice.

19. I use this same analysis in making the case for Schweitzer's educational importance. For instance, the common criticism, made toward the end of his life, of his hospital's obsolete technology and deficient hygiene, or his colonialism or purported racist attitudes, should not detract from his symbolic importance and inspiration to those who carry out the work of educating others. Even as we acknowledge his faults or shortcomings, or attribute them to his own cultural lenses, Schweitzer remains a powerful model for teaching and learning.

20. Henry Clark, *The Ethical Mysticism of Albert Schweitzer* (Boston: Beacon, 1962), 77, cited in Ice, 24. See also Oskar Kraus, *Albert Schweitzer: His Work*

and His Philosophy. Introduction by A. D. Lindsay, trans. E. G. McCalman (London: Adams and Charles Black, 1944), 126f. Hereafter Kraus.

21. *Quest,* quoted in Kraus, 53.
22. Cited by Marvin Meyer in "Affirming Reverence for Life," 28.
23. Ara Paul Barsam, *Reverence for Life: Albert Schweitzer's Great Contribution to Ethical Thought* (New York: Oxford University Press, 2008), 5. Hereafter Barsam, *Reverence for Life.*
24. Cited in Ice, 25. Albert Schweitzer, *Geschichte der Lebens-Jesu-Forschung* (Mohr, Germany: 2nd ed., 1913), 635.
25. Albert Schweitzer, *The Primeval Forest* (Including *On the Edge of the Primeval Forest* and *More from the Primeval Forest*), foreword by William H. Foege (Baltimore and London: Johns Hopkins University Press, 1998) (originally published 1931), 11. Hereafter *Primeval Forest.*
26. *Luke* 16: 19–31: "There was a rich man who was clothed in purple and fine linen and who feasted sumptuously every day. And at his gate lay a poor man named Lazarus, full of sores, who desired to be fed with what fell from the rich man's table; moreover the dogs came and licked his sores. The poor man died and was carried by the angels to Abraham's bosom. The rich man also died and was buried; and in Hades, being in torment, he lifted up his eyes, and saw Abraham far off and Lazarus in his bosom. And he called out 'Father Abraham, have mercy on me, and send Lazarus to dip the end of his finger in water and cool my tongue; for I am in anguish in this flame.' But Abraham said, 'Son, remember that you in your lifetime received your good things, and Lazarus in like manner evil things; but now he is comforted here, and you are in anguish. And besides all this, between us and you a great chasm has been fixed, in order that those who would pass from here to you may not be able, and none may cross from there to us.' And he said, 'Then I beg you, father, to send him to my father's house, for I have five brothers, so that he may warn them, lest they also come into this place of torment.' But Abraham said, 'they have Moses and the prophets; let them hear them.' And he said, 'No, father Abraham; but if some one goes to them from the dead, they will repent.' He said to him, 'If they do not hear Moses and the prophets, neither will they be convinced if some one should rise from the dead.'"
27. *Primeval Forest,* 11.
28. Kraus, 8–9.
29. See especially Chapter 3, "The Voyage to India," in Barsam, *Reverence for Life,* for a critical discussion of how he believed Schweitzer selectively used Indian thought to affirm some of his prejudices.
30. Ara Paul Barsam, "Schweitzer, Jainism, and Reverence for Life," in Meyer and Bergel, *Reverence for Life,* 208.
31. Ibid., 212.
32. Ibid., 239.
33. Ibid., 239–240.
34. Kraus, 42–43.

Chapter 3

1. As Rebecca Earle notes, "Personal letters, particularly those written with no apparent thought to publication, have often been read as windows into the soul of the author. The ancient trope that views the letter as merely a conversation in writing lent particular force to this idea, whereby the letter becomes as unmediated and as unmeditated as a casual conversation. At its best, eighteenth-century epistolary epicures proclaimed, a letter should resemble a conversation between friends. Reading other people's mail thus becomes a form of eavesdropping." Rebecca Earle, "Introduction: letters, writers, and historians," in *Epistolary Selves: letters and letter-writers, 1600–1945*, ed. Rebecca Earle (Aldershot, UK: Ashgate Publishing Limited, 1999), 5.

2. Rhena Schweitzer Miller and Gustav Woytt, eds., *The Albert Schweitzer-Hélène Bresslau Letters 1902–1912*, trans. from the German and ed. Antje Bultmann Lemke, assistant editor Nancy Stewart (Syracuse, NY: Syracuse University Press, 2003), xii. Hereafter *Letters*.

3. Albert Schweitzer, *Essential Writings*. Selected with an Introduction by James Brabazon (Maryknoll, NY: Orbis, 2005), 15. Hereafter *EW*. Compare Brabazon's comment here to how Mike W. Martin characterizes the relationship revealed by the letters: "The letters reveal a relationship of intimate friendship that grew into love during ten years prior to their marriage, when it was first consummated. A deep understanding emerged between them that traditional domesticity was not Albert's calling. Initially they planned to sustain their love as each of them pursued an independent life of service, although gradually they came to realize that Lambaréné offered the promise of shared service as a married couple. It came as a tragedy, to both of them, when Hélène's health proved insufficient for work under the harsh jungle conditions. Judging from Schweitzer's expression of gratitude to her, Hélène released him to continue the work in which she too was deeply invested. If she had not done so, what might have happened? A divisive and angry divorce would have been devastating, but so would abandonment of the mission they both cherished. There are no rules to dictate the obligatory response to genuine dilemmas of this sort." Mike W. Martin, *Albert Schweitzer's Reverence for Life: Ethical Idealism and Self-Realization* (Aldershot, UK: Ashgate, 2007), 20–21. Hereafter Martin, *Reverence for Life*.

4. Denise de Costa, *Anne Frank and Etty Hillesum: Inscribing Spirituality and Sexuality*, trans. Mischa F. C. Hoyinck and Robert C. Chesal (New Brunswick, NJ: Rutgers University Press, 1998), 28.

5. David T. Hansen, *Exploring the Moral HeART of Teaching: Toward a Teacher's Creed* (New York: Teachers College Press, 2001), 178–87.

6. *Letters*, 4

7. Ibid., 5, emphasis added.

8. Ibid., xxvii.

9. Ibid., 7.

10. Ibid., 14.

11. Ibid., 22.
12. Ibid., 24.
13. Ibid., 24–25.
14. Ibid., 32–33. In considering the educational legacy of Schweitzer, this utterance of his disdain for the professorial life appears ironic. Schweitzer felt constricted by the rote and pedantic teaching and learning that were expected of him. Here teaching and learning is removed from action in the world, from things that matter. If we contrast this view to his latter pronouncement that "the school will be the way," we see that he had a clear if not fully articulated idea of what education should be, which I develop in Part II.
15. Ibid., 42–43.
16. Ibid., 46.
17. Ibid., 53–54.
18. Ibid., 56–57.
19. Ibid., 56.
20. Ibid., 57.
21. Ibid., 58.
22. Ibid., 58–59.
23. Ibid., 65.
24. Ibid.
25. Ibid., 64.
26. Charles R. Joy and Melvin Arnold, *The Africa of Albert Schweitzer* (New York: Harper and Brothers, 1948), 11.
27. *Letters*, 67.
28. Ibid.
29. Ibid., 73.
30. Ibid., 84.
31. Ibid., 85.
32. Ibid., 73.
33. Ibid., 83.
34. Ibid., 80–81.
35. Ibid., 79.
36. Ibid., 89.
37. Ibid., 91.
38. Ibid., 94.
39. Ibid., 74.
40. Ibid., 81.
41. Ibid., 96, emphasis added.
42. Ibid., 99.
43. Ibid., 102–103.
44. Ibid., 109.
45. Ibid., 92.
46. In many places Hélène functions for Schweitzer as a sounding board for his ideas, but he realizes that she is carefully and actively listens. She shows this active care in the way that she remembers what he says and presents her own

thoughts. Listening well is a moral act as well as a finely tuned skill. I have been involved for several years with a group of scholars who explore the philosophical and pedagogical aspects of listening, and we have produced numerous conference presentations and papers. For essays by this group, see the special issues of *Learning Inquiry* 1(2) August 2007, and *Teachers College Record* 113(10) October 2011, (http://www.tcrecord.org/Issue.asp?volyear=2011&number=10&volume=113).

47. *Letters*, 180.
48. Ibid., 99.
49. Ibid., 111f.
50. Ibid., 114.
51. Ibid., 114.
52. Ibid., 145f.
53. Ibid., 148.
54. Ibid., 139.
55. Ibid., 169. Themes of compassion resonate in Wagner's opera.
56. Ibid., 183.
57. Ibid., 199–200.
58. Ibid., 220.
59. See Hermann Hagedorn, *Prophet in the Wilderness: The Story of Albert Schweitzer* (New York: Macmillan, 1948), 140–41: Hereafter Hagedorn.
60. The idea of development in education would of course come later with Piaget. Jean Piaget remarks upon Comenius: "How many schools invoke the ideas of development, interest, spontaneous activity, etc., though, in real fact, the only development is that laid down in the curriculum, the only interests are imposed, and the only activities suggested by adult authority! The true measure of active teaching (a form of education that is perhaps almost as rare today as in the seventeenth century) appears to, be the way in which truth is established. There is no authentic activity so long as the pupil accepts the truth of an assertion merely because it is conveyed from an adult to a child, with all the aura of explicit or implicit authority attached to the teachers words or those of the textbooks; but there is activity when the pupil rediscovers or reconstructs truth by means of external, or internal mental, action consisting in experiment or independent reasoning. This all-important fact appears to me to have been clearly grasped by Comenius" (p. 7, Jean Piaget, 'Jan Amos Comenius' (1592–1670). *Prospects (UNESCO, International Bureau of Education)*, vol. XXIII, no. 1/2, 1993, 173–96. Retrieved February 21, 2009, from http://www.ibe.unesco.org/publications/ThinkersPdf/comeniuse.PDF.

Chapter 4

1. Albert Schweitzer, *Out of My Life and Thought: An Autobiography*, trans. Antje Bultmann Lemke (Baltimore and London: Johns Hopkins University Press, 1998), 115. Hereafter *OOMLAT*.

2. David T. Hansen, *The Call to Teach* (New York: Teachers College Press, 1995). Hereafter Hansen.
3. Ibid., xiii.
4. Ibid., xiv.
5. Ibid., 3.
6. Ibid., 11–12.
7. Ibid., 114.
8. The theory and early practice of The North Carolina Center for the Advancement of Teaching are discussed in Anthony G. Rud, Jr., and Walter P. Oldendorf, eds., *A Place for Teacher Renewal: Challenging the Intellect, Creating Educational Reform* (1992; repr., Charlotte, NC: Information Age Publishing, 2008).
9. As Jo and Walter Munz note, "Lembareni, in the galoa language of Gabon, literally means: we want to try, in a sense of an experiment." Jo and Walter Munz, *Albert Schweitzer's Lambaréné: A Legacy of Humanity for Our World Today*, trans. and ed. from the French edition by Patti M. Marxsen (Houston, TX: Penobscot Press/Alondra Press, 2010) (first published in German, 2005, and in French, 2007), 17.
10. Hansen, 124–26.
11. Ibid., 126.
12. Ibid., 126.
13. Ibid., 14–15.
14. The newly translated volume by Jo and Walter Munz, *Albert Schweitzer's Lambaréné*, provides both a wealth of firsthand accounts of the hospital in later years, and as the back cover text states, a historical account "situated in the larger context of Gabon's transformation into a sovereign nation."
15. I draw upon two translations for the following: Albert Schweitzer, *Memoirs of Childhood and Youth*, trans. C. T. Bergel (New York: Macmillan, 1931) (first published in English, 1924). I use this translation in the citations that follow: Albert Schweitzer, *Memoirs of Childhood and Youth*, trans. Kurt Bergel and Alice R. Bergel (Syracuse NY: Syracuse University Press, 1997). Hereafter *Memoirs*.
16. *Memoirs*, 79.
17. Ibid., 81.
18. Ibid., 81.
19. Ibid., 81–82.
20. I am indebted to my former colleague Jerry L. Peters for the following saying: Children are the living messages we send to a time we will not see. As he explains further: "Children are our most precious resource that we have and we must make sure that we have prepared them for the challenges they will face in a global society. As parents, teachers, and teacher educators, we must continually ask ourselves if we are providing them with the appropriate messages. We also need to make sure we look back to our past and ask what messages were given to us by our parents and their parents before them. Through our actions we are living many of the messages we want our children to take with them." Personal correspondence, April 13, 2010.

21. *Memoirs*, 83.
22. Ibid., 83–84.
23. Ibid., 84.
24. Ibid., 87.
25. Darrell J. Fasching, "Beyond Values: Story, Character, and Public Policy," in *Ethics and Decision Making in Local Schools*, ed. James L. Paul et al. (Baltimore: Paul H. Brookes, 1997), 99–122.
26. Anthony G. Rud, Jr., "Learning in Comfort: Developing an Ethos of Hospitality in Education," in *The Educational Conversation: Closing the Gap*, ed. Jim Garrison and Anthony G. Rud, Jr. (Albany: State University of New York Press, 1995), 119–28.
27. *Memoirs*, 89.
28. Ibid., 89–90.
29. Ibid., 91.
30. Ibid.
31. Ibid.
32. Ibid., 93.
33. Ibid., 94–95.
34. Ibid., 95.

Chapter 5

1. Albert Schweitzer, *Out of My Life and Thought: An Autobiography*, trans. Antje Bultmann Lemke (Baltimore and London: Johns Hopkins University Press, 1998), 115., 201–4. Hereafter *OOMLAT*.
2. Albert Schweitzer, "Civilization and Ethics," in *The Philosophy of Civilization*, trans. C. T. Campion (Amherst, NY: Prometheus, 1987).
3. *OOMLAT*, 204.
4. Ibid., 146.
5. Jackson Lee Ice, "Is 'Reverence for Life' a Viable Ethic?," in Ice, *Albert Schweitzer: Sketches for a Portrait* (Lanham, MD: University Press of America, 1994), 37–42. Hereafter Ice.
6. See Ara Paul Barsam, *Reverence for Life: Albert Schweitzer's Great Contribution to Ethical Thought* (New York: Oxford University Press, 2008), 132. Hereafter Barsam, *Reverence for Life*. In discussing some current thinkers on life or ecological ethics, and how they criticized Schweitzer's lack of systematic development for reverence for life, Barsam says, "Schweitzer offers *reverence* as a banner or touchstone—and perhaps should have done more to prevent it from being taken for more, i.e. a practical, one-stop guide in all circumstances." (Italics in original)
7. *OOMLAT*, 225.
8. Ibid., 225–26.
9. Ibid., 154.
10. Ibid., 155.

11. Though Schweitzer claimed that Reverence for Life came to him as an epiphany on the river, Ara Paul Barsam makes a case that study, thinking, and action over a long period of time (and influenced by Indian thought) led Schweitzer to that flash of insight, in Barsam, *Reverence for Life*, Chapter 3 "The Voyage to India." The role of epiphanic insight in contrast to deliberative or meditative thought in determining one's course of action is discussed in Tracy Kidder's book on Dr. Paul Farmer, a contemporary figure often compared to Schweitzer. See Tracy Kidder, *Mountains Beyond Mountains* (New York: Random House, 2003), especially Chapter 8, "The Tin Roofs of Cange."

12. *OOMLAT*, 157, emphasis added.

13. Ibid., 182.

14. Paul Woodruff, *Reverence: Renewing a Forgotten Virtue* (New York: Oxford University Press, 2001), 63. Hereafter Woodruff.

15. Ibid., 7.

16. Ibid., 65.

17. It is beyond the scope of this book to develop the link between reverence and what the German philosopher Martin Heidegger called "*Sein zum Tode*," being toward death. Woodruff speaks of reverence for objects that remind us of human limitation, and that ultimate limitation is death.

18. Neil Postman, *Amusing Ourselves to Death: Public Discourse in the Age of Show Business* (New York: Penguin, 1986).

19. Schweitzer discusses the rupture between Reverence for Life and a Nature that does not recognize this thought, a Nature of waterfalls and tornadoes, both awe-inspiring and destructive at once, in his sermons on Reverence for Life given in Strasbourg's Saint Nicolai Church in 1919. See a detailed philosophical discussion of these sermons in J. Claude Evans, *With Respect for Nature: Living as Part of the Natural World* (Albany: State University of New York Press, 2005), 49–54. This rupture is also evident in that, while Reverence for Life recognizes every life as sacred, life can only exist at the cost of other life. See Predag Cicovacki, ed. *Albert Schweitzer's Ethical Vision: A Sourcebook* (New York: Oxford University Press, 2009), 20.

20. I am indebted to Patti Marxsen for this insight.

21. Robert Payne, *The Three Worlds of Albert Schweitzer* (New York: Thomas Nelson and Sons, 1957), 131. The tragic sense of life is recognized by Schweitzer in the moral neutrality of nature, but he counters this with affirmation: "His theory of ethical optimism is not verifiable but is a postulate or demand of the will-to-live that claims for itself knowledge independent of empirical sources." Ara Paul Barsam, "Schweitzer, Jainism, and Reverence for Life," in *Reverence for Life: The Ethics of Albert Schweitzer for the Twenty-First Century,* ed. Marvin Meyer and Kurt Bergel (Syracuse, NY: Syracuse University Press, 2002), 221–22. Hereafter Meyer and Bergel.

22. Martin Heidegger, "Building, Dwelling, Thinking" in *Poetry, Language, Thought,* trans. Albert Hofstadter (New York: Harper Colophon, 1971) http://evans-experientialism.freewebspace.com/heidegger7a.htm.

23. Ice, 39.

24. Anthony G. Rud, Jr., "Breaking the Egg Crate," *Educational Theory* 43(1) (1993): 71–83.
25. There is only one mention of Schweitzer in Dewey's collected works. Though Schweitzer wanted to meet Dewey during his trip to Aspen, Colorado, in 1949, I have not found evidence that they in fact met.
26. See especially Steven C. Rockefeller, *John Dewey: Religious Faith and Democratic Humanism* (New York: Columbia University Press, 1991). I am indebted to Jim Garrison for discussion of Dewey's religious humanism, especially the idea of natural piety.
27. John Dewey, *The Later Works, Volume 9,* in the *Collected Works of John Dewey,* ed. J. A. Boydston (Carbondale: Southern Illinois University Press, 1986), 19.
28. *OOMLAT,* 184–85.
29. Ibid., 201.
30. Martin, *Reverence for Life,* 99.
31. Ibid., 19.
32. Jean-Jacques Rousseau, *Émile, or On Education,* trans. Allan Bloom (New York: Basic Books, 1979), 37.

Chapter 6

1. Gail F. Melson, *Why the Wild Things Are: Animals in the Lives of Children* (Cambridge, MA: Harvard University Press, 2001).
2. Ara Paul Barsam, *Reverence for Life: Albert Schweitzer's Great Contribution to Ethical Thought* (New York: Oxford University Press, 2008), 89. Hereafter Barsam, *Reverence for Life.*
3. "Quest," 283–84, italics in original, cited in ibid., 90.
4. See Arthur Chickering, Jon Dalton, and Liesa Stamm, *Encouraging Authenticity and Spirituality in Higher Education* (New York: John Wiley, 2006), 205. The Quaker practice of listening attentively is discussed in the concept of "clearness committees" where a small group helps a single person to discover wisdom.
5. The No Child Left Behind Act was signed into law in January 2002. For a critique of high-stakes accountability, see Sharon L. Nichols and David C. Berliner, *Collateral Damage: How High-Stakes Testing Corrupts American Schools* (Cambridge, MA.: Harvard Education Press, 2007). Hereafter Nichols and Berliner.
6. John Dewey, *Democracy and Education. John Dewey: The Middle Works, Volume 9,* ed. Jo Ann Boydston (Carbondale: Southern Illinois University Press, 1916/1980), 8.
7. Paul Woodruff, *Reverence: Renewing a Forgotten Virtue* (New York: Oxford University Press, 2001), 180. Hereafter Woodruff.
8. Jim Garrison points to the eponymous lead character of the film "Forrest Gump" in noting that comedic and often touching aspect of the character's ability to do well without being able to articulate, or even at times understand, his actions make up the core of the film.

9. Katherine Schultz, "After the Blackbird Whistles: Listening to Silence in Classrooms," *Teachers College Record* 113(10) (October 2011), http://www.tcrecord.org/Issue.asp?volyear=2011&number=10&volume=113.

10. See Woodruff, 135: "Ritual is more robust than belief and has more staying power, but wherever there is ritual, there must be the reverence to take that ritual seriously." The "staying power" of ritual comes from its predictability and familiarity to a community. For instance, my former student Hollie Kulago told me that the members of the Diné (Navajo) community know why a mentor is appointed to tie the hair of a girl upon puberty. This ritualistic act signals to the community that this young girl is now at an important point in her life and is due respect from members of the community.

11. H. G. Bissinger, *Friday Night Lights: A Town, a Team, and a Dream* (1990; repr., Cambridge, MA.: Da Capo Press, 2000), 128–29.

12. I owe this example to Jim Garrison.

13. Schultz, "After the Blackbird Whistles."

14. Woodruff, 193.

15. A. G. Rud and Alan M. Beck, "Kids and Critters in Class Together," *Phi Delta Kappan* 82(4) (2000): 313–15.

16. Anthony G. Rud, Jr., "Building a Rationale for Teacher Renewal," in *A Place for Teacher Renewal: Challenging the Intellect, Creating Educational Reform,* ed. Anthony G. Rud, Jr., and Walter P. Oldendorf (1992; repr., Charlotte, NC: Information Age Publishing, 2008). Hereafter Rud and Oldendorf..

17. R. Bruce McPherson, "Administration for Human and Organizational Growth," in Rud and Oldendorf, 88–90.

18. Herman Melville, *Moby-Dick; or, the Whale.* http://www.readprint.com/work-1207/Herman-Melville.

19. Woodruff, 132.

20. Ibid., 117.

21. Thomas J. Sergiovanni, *The Lifeworld of Leadership: Creating Culture, Community, and Personal Meaning in Our Schools* (San Francisco: Jossey-Bass, 1999). Hereafter Sergiovanni.

22. Ibid., 17.

23. Ibid.

24. Terrence E. Deal and Kent D. Peterson, *Shaping School Culture: The Heart of Leadership* (San Francisco: Jossey-Bass, 1999), 37. Hereafter Deal and Peterson.

25. Ibid., 23.

26. Ibid., 31.

27. Ibid., 32.

28. Ibid., 36.

29. Sergiovanni, 168.

30. Albert Schweitzer, *The Primeval Forest* (Baltimore: Johns Hopkins University Press, 1998), 128.

31. Deal and Peterson, 34.

32. Many teachers express a profound sense of loss and grief at the end of the school year, especially at commencement exercises.
33. Woodruff, 19.
34. Deal and Peterson, 123–24.
35. Ibid., 86.

Chapter 7

1. Albert Schweitzer, *Out of My Life and Thought: An Autobiography,* trans. Antje Bultmann Lemke (Baltimore and London: Johns Hopkins University Press, 1998), 201. Hereafter *OOMLAT.*
2. Ibid., 227.
3. Ibid., 232.
4. I am indebted to John Pomery for discussion of these ideas.
5. While acknowledging the extremity of his commitment, Mike W. Martin ingeniously calls Schweitzer's commitment and his "ethical mysticism" another kind of "invisible hand" and contrasts it to Adam Smith: "Schweitzer's writing sparkles with metaphors of moral unity, of invisible hands quite different than Smith had in mind." Mike W. Martin, *Meaningful Work: Rethinking Professional Ethics* (New York: Oxford University Press, 2000), 16–17.
6. Thomas Donaldson, *The Ethics of International Business* (New York: Oxford University Press, 1991).
7. Mark Johnson, *Moral Imagination: Implications of Cognitive Science for Ethics* (Chicago: University of Chicago Press, 1993).
8. James R. Rest, Muriel J. Bebeau, Mickie Bebeau, Darcia Narvaez, and Stephen J. Thoma, *Postconventional Moral Thinking: A Neo-Kohlbergian Approach* (Mahwah, NJ: Lawrence Erlbaum Associates, 1999).
9. Patti Marxsen informed me that "the original hospital was established in 1913 and rebuilt in 1924. In 1927, Schweitzer moved to a larger site 3 kilometers north and created a new facility. Finally, in 1981, a modern hospital was built up the hill from the 1927 hospital, which has now become part of a 'Zone Historique' that includes numerous renovated buildings and a museum." Personal communication with Patti Marxsen, March 15, 2006.
10. *OOMLAT,* 92.
11. Ibid., 85–86.
12. Ibid., 88.
13. See John Gunther, *Inside Africa* (New York: Harper and Brothers, 1955), Chapter 35, "A Visit to Dr. Albert Schweitzer," 712–34. While acknowledging Gunther's observations about the conditions at Lambaréné, Norman Cousins notes "It is not without significance that there wasn't a single epidemic in all the years the Schweitzer hospital had been in existence. Research specialists interested in epidemiology found abundant evidence at the Schweitzer hospital that the traditional notions of sanitation were not as important as

the circumstances under which a human being becomes ill." Norman Cousins, "How Albert Schweitzer Exerted His Power," *Washington University Magazine*, Spring 1975, 32.

14. With the contributions, Schweitzer used what they gave in return to feed and support others, and noted, "Experience has confirmed the educational value of some form of payment." *OOMLAT*, 140.

15. J. F. Montague, *The Why of Albert Schweitzer* (New York: Hawthorn Books, 1965), 49. Hereafter Montague.

16. Ibid., 221.

17. Norman Cousins, *Dr. Schweitzer of Lambaréné* (New York: Harper and Row, 1960).

18. Anthony G. Rud, Jr., "Learning in Comfort. Developing an Ethos of Hospitality in Education," in *The Educational Conversation: Closing the Gap*, ed. James W. Garrison and Anthony G. Rud, Jr. (Albany: State University of New York Press, 1995), 119–28.

19. Sergiovanni's distinction, borrowed from Jürgen Habermas, between *lifeworld* and *systemsworld* practices is discussed in Chapter 6. These lifeworld practices include ritual and ceremony, also discussed in that chapter as aspects of practical reverence.

20. James Brabazon, *Albert Schweitzer: A Biography*, second edition (Syracuse, NY: Syracuse University Press, 2000), 13. Hereafter Brabazon.

21. Ibid., 153.

22. Ann Hartle, *Michel de Montaigne: Accidental Philosopher* (New York: Cambridge University Press, 2003).

23. I am indebted to John M. Kirby for discussion of Aristotle.

24. Aristotle, *Rhetoric* 1366B: 17–18.

25. Brabazon, p. 76.

26. Albert Schweitzer, *The Primeval Forest* (Including *On the Edge of the Primeval Forest* and *More from the Primeval Forest*), foreword by William H. Foege (Baltimore and London: Johns Hopkins University Press, 1998) (originally published 1931), 128. Hereafter *Primeval Forest*.

27. David T. Hansen, *The Call to Teach* (New York: Teachers College Press, 1995), 139.

28. Ibid.

29. Brabazon, 76–77.

30. Schweitzer in Cousins, *Dr. Schweitzer of Lambaréné*, 125.

31. *OOMLAT*, 154.

32. Ibid., 157.

33. Ibid., 223.

34. Ibid., 225–26.

35. Ann Cotrell Free, ed., *Animals, Nature & Albert Schweitzer*. http://www.awionline. org/schweitzer/as-idx.htm, 1982, 18. Hereafter Free.

36. Brabazon, 147–48.

37. John Dewey, *Experience and Nature*. In *The Later Works, 1925–1953: Vol. 1*, ed. JoAnn Boydston (Carbondale: Southern Illinois University Press, 1981), 34.

38. Walter Munz, "Reverence for Life at Lambaréné in Albert Schweitzer's last years," Trans. Patti M. Marxsen, paper presented at The Ethics of Reverence for Life Colloquium, Strasbourg, France, November 2005.

39. John Dewey, *The Quest for Certainty*. In *The Later Works, 1925–1953: Vol. 4*, ed. JoAnn Boydston (Carbondale: Southern Illinois University Press, 1981), 110–11.

40. "Learning in Comfort," 119.

41. Ibid., 121.

42. Ibid., 122.

43. *OOMLAT*, 211.

44. Montague, 49.

45. W. E. B. Du Bois, "The Black Man and Albert Schweitzer" in *The Albert Schweitzer Jubilee Book*, ed. A. A. Roback, *The Albert Schweitzer Jubilee Book* (Cambridge, MA: Sci-Art Publishers, 1945), 126.

46. *Primeval Forest*, 95.

47. Personal communication with David T. Hansen, March 15, 2006.

48. Jane Roland Martin, *The Schoolhome: Rethinking Schools for Changing Families* (Cambridge, MA: Harvard University Press, 1992), 41.

49. Ibid., 12.

50. Norman Cousins, *Dr. Schweitzer of Lambaréné* (New York: Harper and Row, 1960), 179.

51. Free, 59.

52. Robert Payne, *The Three Worlds of Albert Schweitzer* (New York: Thomas Nelson and Sons, 1957), 150.

53. Brabazon, 330–40.

Chapter 8

1. Bassek ba Kobhio (Director), *Le Grand Blanc de Lambaréné* [Motion Picture]. San Francisco: California Newsreel, 1995.

2. Harry Targ used this term, commenting on a reevaluation of Paul Robeson's social activism, at an American Studies colloquium at Purdue University.

3. Jerome C. Hill (Director and Producer) and Erica Anderson (Producer), *Albert Schweitzer*. [Motion Picture]. Los Angeles: Louis de Rouchemont Associates, 1957.

4. I borrow the term *excavation* from Paul C. Taylor, "Art, Education, and Witness; or, How to Make Our Ideals Clear," in *Philosophy of Education 2009*, ed. Deborah Kerdeman et. al. (Urbana, IL: Philosophy of Education Society, 2010), 26. Taylor speaks of self-excavation as a moral enterprise.

5. Sandra Brennan, writing for the *All Movie Guide* and reproduced on the *New York Times* Web site below, breezily dismisses Schweitzer, though she misspells the name of the country where he worked: "This African comedy takes a sharp, satiric poke at one of the white colonialist's most sacred cows—the humanitarian work of Dr. Albert Schweitzer. The film was shot beside Ganon's

(sic) Ogooué River in Lambaréné, where the real Schweitzer did most of his work, and the settings are more realistic than romanticized. The story covers the last 25 years in the Great White's African stay, and observes the changing African attitudes towards the good doctor's frequently condescending ministrations." http://movies.nytimes.com/movie/134695/Le-Grand-Blanc-de-Lambarene/overview.

6. Francis Higginson, "The Well-Tempered Savage: Albert Schweitzer, Music, and Imperial Deafness," *Research in African Literatures* 36, 5 (2005): 205–22.

7. Compare this pronouncement with a similar view from Toni Morrison: Schweitzer "didn't care anything about those Africans. They could have been rats. He was in a laboratory testing *himself*." Toni Morrison, *Song of Solomon* (New York: New American Library), 157, cited in Mike W. Martin, *Albert Schweitzer's Reverence for Life: Ethical Idealism and Self-Realization* (Aldershot UK: Ashgate Publishing Limited, 2007), 50. Hereafter Martin, *Reverence for Life.* Martin shares a contrasting story from the account of Edgar Berman, who served as a surgeon at Lambaréné in 1960. A pygmy woman called Mama San Nom ("No Name") was allowed to "roam freely at the hospital, naked and unkempt. In return, she helped other patients by babysitting or cooking. Patients accepted her, even though she was not a member of their tribes. Schweitzer expressed concern and interest, suggesting she might have something to teach about independence, generosity, and transcending tribalism." Edgar Berman, *In Africa with Schweitzer* (New York: Harper and Row, 1986), 62–66, cited in Martin, *Reverence for Life,* 56.

8. J. F. Montague, *The Why of Albert Schweitzer* (New York: Hawthorn Books, 1965), 91–92. Hereafter Montague.

9. The Schweitzer legend grew in the popular press even as sympathetic critics, such as John Gunther, and less sympathetic ones, such as Gerald McKnight, published critical accounts of Lambaréné. For a detailed discussion of a widely read *Life* magazine spread on Schweitzer that appeared on November 15, 1954, see Jessica Levin, "In the Heart of Sickness: A *Life* Portrait of Dr. Albert Schweitzer," in *Images of Africa: Stereotypes and Realities,* ed. Daniel Mengara (Trenton, NJ: Africa World Press, 2001), 237–48.

10. I owe this idea to Raymond D. Boisvert, who argues that we must rethink the legacy of John Dewey for our time. See his *John Dewey: Rethinking Our Time* (Albany: State University of New York Press, 1997).

11. Martin, *Reverence for Life,* 84.

12. With typical directness, Schweitzer discusses colonization "as a peasant talks of his cabbages, and not as an artist or a poet would depict the same cabbages." He sees it as a moral duty of the state to "correct, by its actions, the evils developed through unrestrained economic advance." Albert Schweitzer, "The Relations of the White and Coloured Races," *The Contemporary Review* CXXXIII, January–June 1928, 65. Certainly Schweitzer was aware of the economic exploitation of central Africa, particularly its timber. See Albert Schweitzer, "Lumbermen and Raftsmen in the Primeval Forest," in Part I, Chapter 6, *The Primeval Forest (Including On the Edge of the Primeval Forest*

and *More from the Primeval Forest*), foreword by William H. Foege (Baltimore and London: Johns Hopkins University Press, 1998) (originally published 1931), Hereafter *Primeval Forest*.

13. Robert Payne, *The Three Worlds of Albert Schweitzer* (New York: Thomas Nelson and Sons, 1957), 178. Hereafter Payne.

14. See the discussion of educational prophecy in David E. Purpel and William M. McLaurin, Jr., *Reflections on the Moral and Spiritual Crisis in Education* (New York: Peter Lang, 2004). Hereafter Purpel and McLaurin.

15. Payne, 240 (italics in original).

16. William Ayers, *Teaching Toward Freedom: Moral Commitment and Ethical Action in the Classroom* (Boston: Beacon Press, 2004), 34.

17. Jim Garrison and Roger Jones, review of *Teaching at the Crossroads of Faith and School: The Teacher as Prophetic Pragmatist*, by Jeffrey Ayala Milligan. *Educational Studies* 37(3) (2005): 289.

18. Purpel and McLaurin, 110.

19. Ibid., 113.

20. Abraham Heschel quoted by David Purpel and cited in David A. Gruenewald, "More Than One Profound Truth: Making Sense of Divergent Criticalities," *Educational Studies*, 37(2) (2005): 213.

21. Jim Garrison, *Dewey and Eros: Wisdom and Desire in the Art of Teaching* (New York: Teachers College Press, 1997), 134. I am indebted to Jeffrey Ayala Milligan for this insight into Garrison's work on teacher as prophet.

22. Karl Jaspers, *Socrates, Buddha, Confucius, Jesus: The Paradigmatic Individuals*, trans. Ralph Manheim (New York: Harcourt, 1962). Hereafter Jaspers.

23. Ibid., 3.

24. Ibid., 87.

25. While it can be illuminating to consider how Schweitzer measures up to the paradigmatic individual, the standard in Jaspers's sense is almost impossibly high. We might instead follow James Brabazon and look at him as a religious genius, or in the very least, use what Brabazon says about this kind of individual to help assess Schweitzer's influence: "If it is the religious or ethical nature of the person which seizes the world of appearances and its events in a corresponding unique unity, one calls it moral or religious genius. Therefore, the nature of every religious genius is shown in that he constructs a unity by working over the wreckage of a religion destroyed either deliberately or unconsciously as the exigencies of his religious personality dictate, without concern as to whether for the average person, the broken pieces do not fit together into a structure or not. The genius seizes only what he needs for his new, unified image, lit by his own light—and the rest becomes blurred in the shade. Thus, for Jesus of Nazareth, only that exists in the Old Testament which proves to be in harmony with his religious talent. It is from here that light is shed: 'On these two hang all the law and the prophets.' Thus Luther, being the religious genius that he was, fits together the most contradictory portions of medieval dogma because he brings a unified principle to bear on it; he voices contractions, but he never felt them." James Brabazon, *Albert*

Schweitzer: A Biography, second edition (Syracuse, NY: Syracuse University Press, 2000), 74.
26. Jaspers, 90.
27. Ibid., 95.

Chapter 9

1. Oskar Kraus, *Albert Schweitzer: His Work and His Philosophy.* Introduction by A. D. Lindsay, trans. E. G. Mc Calman (London: Adams and Charles Black, 1944), viii. Hereafter Kraus.
2. Ibid., 1.
3. Albert Schweitzer, *The Primeval Forest* (Including *On the Edge of the Primeval Forest* and *More from the Primeval Forest*), foreword by William H. Foege (Baltimore and London: Johns Hopkins University Press, 1998) (originally published 1931), 11.
4. Ibid.
5. Kraus, 10f, looks to the memoirs for evidence of further motivation, and surmises that Schweitzer was a sensitive youth who needed to overcome crushing pessimism.
6. Don DeLillo, *White Noise* (New York: Viking Penguin, 1985).
7. Gene V Glass, *Fertilizers, Pills, and Magnetic Strips: The Fate of Public Education in America* (Charlotte, NC: Information Age Publishing, 2008), xii.
8. David C. Berliner and Bruce J. Biddle, *The Manufactured Crisis: Myths, Fraud, and the Attack on America's Public Schools* (New York: Basic Books, 1996).
9. Sharon L. Nichols and David C. Berliner, *Collateral Damage: How High-Stakes Testing Corrupts American Schools.* Cambridge, MA: Harvard Education Press, 2007.
10. Jackson Lee Ice, *Albert Schweitzer: Sketches for a Portrait* (Lanham, MD: University Press of America, 1994), 44. Hereafter Ice.
11. Johann Heinrich Pestalozzi, cited in Kate Silber, *Pestalozzi: The Man and His Work* (3rd edition) (New York: Schocken Books, 1973), 136.
12. David C. King, Frances Daniels-Thompson, and Ann Hanchett Boland, *An Albert Schweitzer Activity Book: Curriculum Guide for Grades 1–6* (Great Barrington, MA: Albert Schweitzer Center, 1992).
13. Charles Rinaldi, *The Albert Schweitzer Inter-School Service Project* (Wallingford, CT: Albert Schweitzer Institute for the Humanities, 1998). Like the Albert Schweitzer Center in Massachusetts, the Albert Schweitzer Institute at the private preparatory school Choate Rosemary Hall no longer exists. The institute's activities were ambitious, including an "international youth congress for community service," though largely unrealized.
14. Nikki Lindberg, "Teaching Reverence for Life," in *Reverence for Life: The Ethics of Albert Schweitzer for the Twenty-First Century,* ed. Marvin Meyer and Kurt Bergel (Syracuse NY: Syracuse University Press, 2002), 271. Hereafter Lindberg.
15. Ibid.

16. Lindberg, 272.

17. Lindberg gives very brief descriptions of the institute's programs that include the trip to Suriname, as well as the more educationally intriguing development of what she calls Action Packs. These were curriculum guides that include an "age-appropriate text about or by Albert Schweitzer, a teacher's guide and discussion questions, and ideas for community service." A teacher reported on the K-2 action pack with its set of activities that included students viewing and analyzing a poster of Schweitzer, reading a picture book about his life, and playing a tape with Schweitzer at the organ playing Bach followed by traditional African music. The anecdotal reports of how the students were affected are touching, such as, "I wish he were alive so he could remind people to be kind." Lindberg, 276–77.

18. Personal communication with the founder of the Harmony Institute, Martha E. Lentz, July 31 and August 7, 2009.

19. Harmony Residential Properties: Restrictions, Guidelines, and Goals Concerning Companion Animals, Habitat and Wildlife. Harmony Foundation, Inc., and Birchwood Acres Limited Partnership LLLP© 2002. All rights reserved.

20. Ibid.

21. Bill Samuels, "Overall Goals of the Compassionate Curriculum," unpublished paper, The Harmony Institute, Harmony FL, 2006.

22. Ibid.

23. "In-Take Questions: Living in Harmony with Nature, A Partnership Program," unpublished document, The Harmony Institute, Harmony FL, 2009.

24. "Falconry Once More," in *The Animal World of Albert Schweitzer: Jungle Insights into Reverence for Life,* ed. and trans. Charles R. Joy (Boston: Beacon Press, 1951), 177. Originally published as "Nochmals Falkenjägerei," *Atlantis* (Zurich), March 1932.

25. "Living in Harmony with Nature Thursday, August 14, 2009—Wildlife," unpublished document, The Harmony Institute, Harmony FL, 2009.

26. "After the war, during my studies in the United States at the University of Chicago, I became acquainted with the endeavors of American education, based on the thoughts of John Dewey." Casparis does not discuss Deweyan educational philosophy or practice in any depth beyond this mention, and a subsequent claim of "educating the whole man, considered both as a free person and as a responsible member of society." Hans Casparis, "The Albert Schweitzer College," in *In Albert Schweitzer's Realm: A Symposium,* ed. A. A. Roback (Cambridge MA.: Sci-Art Publishers, 1962), 383, 385.

27. The Albert Schweitzer Institute at Chapman University sponsored a conference, "Albert Schweitzer at the Turn of the Millennium," in February 1999 and talks given at that time are included with other essays on Schweitzer's work, as well as some of Schweitzer's writings, in Meyer and Bergel. In October 2005, the Albert Schweitzer Institute at Quinnipiac University sponsored a conference, "Reverence for Life Revisited: Albert Schweitzer's Relevance Today," with a keynote speech by Jane Goodall, that resulted *in Reverence for Life Revisited: Albert Schweitzer's Relevance Today,* ed. David Ives and David A. Valone.

28. Joie Karnes, Maria Tafoya, Timothy Johnson, Marianne Tardaguila, and Anna Blishak Peschong, "Student Essays on Albert Schweitzer and Reverence for Life," in Meyer and Bergel, 282–306. Hereafter Karnes et. al.

29. "Student Essays on Albert Schweitzer and Reverence for Life," in Meyer and Bergel, 282.

30. Karnes et al., 285.

31. Ibid., 286–87.

32. See http://www.quinnipiac.edu/x299.xml.

33. John Miller, "A Schweitzer Approach to Higher Education: Utilizing Principles Drawn from the Life of Albert Schweitzer to Develop a Holistic and Comprehensive Educational Model," (unpublished MA thesis, Augsburg College, 2008), 8–9.

34. In addition to the examples cited here, others have drawn upon Schweitzer to enact classroom practices. Sonia MacPherson talks about establishing classrooms as "sanctuaries for Life," by which a classroom becomes "a focal point for teaching applied ethics in context through the cultivation of non-harm and compassion." Sonia MacPherson, "Learning Our Relations: *Teaching reverence for living beings*," paper presented at the Global, Environmental and Outdoor Education Committee conference, Edmonton, Alberta, May 2–5, 2002, 4.

35. Albert Schweitzer, *Out of My Life and Thought: An Autobiography*, trans. Antje Bultmann Lemke (Baltimore and London: Johns Hopkins University Press, 1998), 28. Hereafter *OOMLAT*.

36. Werner Picht, *The Life and Thought of Albert Schweitzer*, trans. Edward Fitzgerald (New York: Harper and Row, 1964), 103.

37. I am indebted to Jack Fenner for this insight.

38. As cited in J. F. Montague, *The Why of Albert Schweitzer* (New York: Hawthorn Books, 1965), 201.

39. David T. Hansen, *Exploring the Moral HeART of Teaching: Toward a Teacher's Creed* (New York, Teachers College Press , 2001), 178.

40. Ibid, 175–78.

41. Ibid, 175–76.

42. Hermann Hagedorn, *Prophet in the Wilderness: The Story of Albert Schweitzer* (New York: Macmillan, 1948), 26, italics added.

43. Robert Bolt, *A Man For All Seasons* (New York: Random House, 1962), 8–9. The oft-quoted lines, rarely cited in context, are below, underlined:

> Sir Thomas More: But, Richard, in office they offer you all sorts of things. I was once offered a whole village, with a mill, and a manor house, and heavens knows what else—a coat of arms, I shouldn't be surprised. <u>Why not be a teacher? You'd be a fine teacher; perhaps a great one.</u>
> Richard Rich: <u>If I was, who would know it?</u>
> Sir Thomas More: <u>You; your pupils; your friends; God. Not a bad public, that . . .</u> Oh, and a *quiet* life.

44. *OOMLAT*, 90.

Bibliography

Abrell, Ron. "Albert Schweitzer: Educator for a Season," *Contemporary Education XLVI* (1) (1974): 28–33.

————. "The School Will Be the Way," *Humane Education* (1978): 10–11.

————. "The Educational Thought of Albert Schweitzer," *The Clearing House 54* (7) (1981): 293–96.

Ayers, William. *Teaching Toward Freedom: Moral Commitment and Ethical Action in the Classroom.* Boston: Beacon Press, 2004.

Barsam, Ara Paul. *Reverence for Life: Albert Schweitzer's Great Contribution to Ethical Thought.* New York: Oxford University Press, 2008.

————. "Schweitzer, Jainism, and Reverence for Life," in *Reverence for Life: The Ethics of Albert Schweitzer for the Twenty-First Century,* edited by Marvin Meyer and Kurt Bergel. Syracuse, NY: Syracuse University Press, 2002, 207–45.

Baur, Hermann. "Albert Schweitzer als Erzieher." *Schweitzerische Lehrerzeitung,* 27/28 (1968).

Beck, Alan M., and Anthony G. Rud, Jr., "Kids and Critters in Class Together," *Phi Delta Kappan* 82(4) (2000): 313–15.

Bekoff, Marc. *The Emotional Lives of Animals: A Leading Scientist Explores Animal Joy, Sorrow, and Empathy—And Why They Matter.* Novato, CA: New World Library, 2007.

———— and Jessica Pierce. *Wild Justice: The Moral Lives of Animals.* Chicago: University of Chicago Press, 2009.

Berliner, David C., and Bruce J. Biddle. *The Manufactured Crisis: Myths, Fraud, and the Attack on America's Public Schools.* New York: Basic Books, 1996.

Bissinger, H. G. *Friday Night Lights: A Town, a Team, and a Dream.* 1990. Reprint Cambridge, MA: Da Capo Press, 2000.

Blackwell, David McClaughry. "Reverence for life as an educational ideal with special reference to the ethical thought of Albert Schweitzer" (MA dissertation, McGill University, 1969) Retrieved January 27, 2008, from ProQuest Digital Dissertations database (Publication No. AAT MK04806).

Boisvert, Raymond D. *John Dewey: Rethinking Our Time.* Albany: State University of New York Press, 1997.

Bolt, Robert. *A Man for All Seasons.* New York: Random House, 1962.

Brabazon, James. *Albert Schweitzer: A Biography.* Second edition. Syracuse, NY: Syracuse University Press, 2000.

Brennan, Sandra. "Le Grand Blanc de Lambaréné." http://movies.nytimes.com/movie/134695/Le-Grand-Blanc-de-Lambarene/overview.

Chickering, Arthur, Jon Dalton, and Liesa Stamm. *Encouraging Authenticity and Spirituality in Higher Education.* New York: John Wiley and Sons, 2006.

Cicovacki, Predag, ed. *Albert Schweitzer's Ethical Vision: A Sourcebook.* New York: Oxford University Press, 2009.

Costa, Denise de. *Anne Frank and Etty Hillesum: Inscribing Spirituality and Sexuality.* Translated by Mischa F. C. Hoyinck and Robert E. Chesal. New Brunswick, NJ: Rutgers University Press, 1998.

Cousins, Norman. *Albert Schweitzer's Mission: Healing and Peace.* New York: W. W. Norton, 1985.

————. *Dr. Schweitzer of Lambaréné.* New York: Harper and Row, 1960.

————. "How Albert Schweitzer Exerted His Power," *Washington University Magazine,* Spring 1975: 31–34.

Dadds, Mark R. "Conduct Problems and Cruelty to Animals in Children: What is the Link?" In *The International Handbook of Animal Abuse and Cruelty: Theory, Research, and Application,* edited by Frank R. Ascione, 111–28. West Lafayette, IN: Purdue University Press, 2008.

Deal, Terrence E., and Kent D. Peterson, *Shaping School Culture: The Heart of Leadership.* San Francisco: Jossey-Bass, 1999.

DeLillo, Don. *White Noise.* New York: Viking Penguin, 1985.

Dewey, John. *Democracy and Education. John Dewey: The Middle Works, Volume 9.* Edited by Jo Ann Boydston. Carbondale: Southern Illinois University Press, 1916/1980.

————. *The Later Works, 1925–1953: Vol. 1.* Edited by Jo Ann Boydston. Carbondale: Southern Illinois University Press, 1981.

————. *The Later Works, 1925–1953: Vols. 4 & 9.* Edited by Jo Ann Boydston. Carbondale: Southern Illinois University Press, 1984, 1986.

Donaldson, Thomas. *The Ethics of International Business.* New York, NY: Oxford University Press, 1991.

DuBois, W. E. B. "The Black Man and Albert Schweitzer." In *The Albert Schweitzer Jubilee Book,* edited by A. A. Roback, 121–27. Cambridge, MA: Sci-Art, 1945.

Earle, Rebecca. "Introduction: letters, writers, and historians," in *Epistolary Selves: letters and letter-writers, 1600–1945,* edited by Rebecca Earle, 1–12. Aldershot, UK: Ashgate, 1999.

Evans, J. Claude. *With Respect for Nature: Living as Part of the Natural World.* Albany: State University of New York Press, 2005.

Fasching, Darrell J., "Beyond Values: Story, Character, and Public Policy," in *Ethics and Decision Making in Local Schools,* edited by James L. Paul, Neal H. Berger, Pamela G. Osnes, Yolanda G. Martinez, and William C. Morse, 99–122. Baltimore: Paul H. Brookes, 1997.

Free, Ann Cotrell, ed. *Animals, Nature & Albert Schweitzer.* http://www.awionline.org/schweitzer/as-idx.htm, 1982.

Garrison, Jim. *Dewey and Eros: Wisdom and Desire in the Art of Teaching*. New York: Teachers College Press, 1997.

Garrison, Jim, and A. G. Rud. "Reverence in Classroom Teaching," *Teachers College Record, 111*(11) (2009): 2626–46.

Garrison, Jim, and Roger Jones. Review of *Teaching at the Crossroads of Faith and School: The Teacher as Prophetic Pragmatist*, by Jeffrey Ayala Milligan. *Educational Studies 37*(3) (2005): 286–90.

Glass, Gene V. *Fertilizers, Pills, and Magnetic Strips: The Fate of Public Education in America*. Charlotte, NC: Information Age Publishing, 2008.

Glickman, Carl D. *Holding Sacred Ground: Essays on Leadership, Courage, and Endurance in Our Schools*. San Francisco: Jossey-Bass, 2003.

Gunther, John. *Inside Africa*. New York: Harper and Brothers, 1955.

Hagedorn, Hermann. *Prophet in the Wilderness: The Story of Albert Schweitzer*. New York: Macmillan, 1948.

Hansen, David T. *The Call to Teach*. New York: Teachers College Press, 1995.

———. *Exploring the Moral HeART of Teaching: Toward a Teacher's Creed*. New York: Teachers College Press, 2001.

Harmony Foundation, Inc., and Birchwood Acres Limited Partnership LLLP. *Harmony Residential Properties: Restrictions, Guidelines, and Goals Concerning Companion Animals, Habitat, and Wildlife*. (Harmony, FL, 2002). All rights reserved.

Hartle, Ann. *Michel de Montaigne: Accidental Philosopher*. New York: Cambridge University Press, 2003.

Heidegger, Martin. "Building, Dwelling, Thinking" in Albert Hofstadter, trans. *Poetry, Language, Thought*. New York: Harper Colophon Books, 1971. http://evans-experientialism.freewebspace.com/heidegger7a.htm.

Higginson, Francis, "The Well-Tempered Savage: Albert Schweitzer, Music, and Imperial Deafness." *Research in African Literatures 36*, 5 (2005): 205–22.

Hill, Jerome C. (Producer and Director) and Erica Anderson (Producer). *Albert Schweitzer* [Motion Picture] (Los Angeles: Louis de Rouchemont Associates, 1957).

Ice, Jackson Lee. *Albert Schweitzer: Sketches for a Portrait*. Lanham, MD: University Press of America, Inc., 1994.

"In-Take Questions: Living in Harmony with Nature, A Partnership Program." Unpublished document. Harmony, FL: The Harmony Institute, 2009.

Ives, David, and David A. Valone, eds. *Reverence for Life Revisited: Albert Schweitzer's Relevance Today*. Newcastle, UK: Cambridge Scholars Publishing, 2007.

Jaspers, Karl. *Socrates, Buddha, Confucius, Jesus: the Paradigmatic Individuals*. Translated by Ralph Manheim. New York: Harcourt, 1962.

Johnson, Mark. *Moral Imagination: Implications of Cognitive Science for Ethics*. Chicago: University of Chicago Press, 1993.

Jonas, Mark E. "A (R)evaluation of Nietzsche's Anti-democratic Pedagogy: The Overman, Perspectivism, and Self-Overcoming," *Studies in Philosophy and Education, 2* (2009): 153–69.

Joy, Charles R., ed. *Albert Schweitzer: An Anthology*. Boston: Beacon Press, 1967.

Joy, Charles R., and Melvin Arnold. *The Africa of Albert Schweitzer*. New York: Harper and Brothers, 1948.

Kidder, Tracy. *Mountains Beyond Mountains*. New York: Random House, 2003.

King, David C., Frances Daniels-Thompson, and Ann Hanchett Boland. *An Albert Schweitzer Activity Book: Curriculum Guide for Grades 1–6*. Great Barrington, MA: Albert Schweitzer Center, 1992.

Kobhio, Bassek ba (Director). *Le Grand Blanc de Lambaréné* [Motion Picture]. San Francisco: California Newsreel, 1995.

Kraus, Oskar. *Albert Schweitzer: His Work and His Philosophy*. Introduction by A. D. Lindsay, Translated by E. G. McCalman. London: Adams and Charles Black, 1944.

Levin, Jessica, "In the Heart of Sickness: A *Life* Portrait of Dr. Albert Schweitzer." In *Images of Africa: Stereotypes and Realities*, edited by Daniel Mengara, 237–48. Trenton, NJ: Africa World Press, 2001.

MacPherson, Sonia, "Learning Our Relations: Teaching reverence for living beings," paper presented at the Global, Environmental and Outdoor Education Committee conference, Edmonton, AB, May 2–5, 2002.

Martin, Jane Roland. *Schoolhome: Rethinking Schools for Changing Families*. Cambridge, MA: Harvard University Press, 1992.

Martin, Mike W. *Albert Schweitzer's Reverence for Life: Ethical Idealism and Self-Realization*. Aldershot, UK: Ashgate, 2007.

———. *Meaningful Work: Rethinking Professional Ethics*. New York: Oxford University Press, 2000.

McKnight, Gerald. *Verdict on Schweitzer: The Man Behind the Legend of Lambaréné*. New York: John Day, 1964.

Melson, Gail F. *Why the Wild Things Are: Animals in the Lives of Children*. Cambridge, MA: Harvard University Press, 2001.

Melville, Herman. *Moby-Dick; or, the Whale*. http://www.readprint.com/work-1207/Herman-Melville.

Meyer, Marvin, and Kurt Bergel, eds. *Reverence for Life: The Ethics of Albert Schweitzer for the Twenty-First Century*. Syracuse, NY: Syracuse University Press, 2002.

Miller, Rhena Schweitzer, and Gustav Woytt, eds. *The Albert Schweitzer-Hélène Bresslau Letters 1902–1912*. Translated from the German and edited by Antje Bultmann Lemke, assistant editor Nancy Stewart. Syracuse, NY: Syracuse University Press, 2003.

Milligan, Jeffrey Ayala. *Teaching at the Crossroads of Faith and School*. New York: University Press of America, 2002.

Montague, J. F. *The Why of Albert Schweitzer*. New York: Hawthorn Books, 1965.

Munz, Walter. "Reverence for Life at Lambaréné in Albert Schweitzer's last years." Translated by Patti M. Marxsen. Paper presented at The Ethics of Reverence for Life Colloquium, Strasbourg, France, November 2005.

Munz, Walter, and Jo Munz. *Albert Schweitzer's Lambaréné: A Legacy of Humanity for Our World Today*. Translated from the French edition by Patti M. Marxsen.

Houston, TX: Penobscot Press/Alondra Press, 2010 (first published in German 2005 and in French 2007).

Nichols, Sharon L., and David C. Berliner. *Collateral Damage: How High-Stakes Testing Corrupts American Schools.* Cambridge, MA: Harvard Education Press, 2007.

Payne, Robert. *The Three Worlds of Albert Schweitzer.* New York: Thomas Nelson, 1957.

Piaget, Jean. "Jan Amos Comenius (1592–1670)." In *Prospects UNESCO, International Bureau of Education,* XXIII(1/2) 1993: 173–96. Retrieved February 21, 2009, from http://www.ibe.unesco.org/publications/ThinkersPdf/comeniuse.PDF.

Picht, Werner. *The Life and Thought of Albert Schweitzer.* Translated by Edward Fitzgerald. New York: Harper and Row, 1964.

Postman, Neil. *Amusing Ourselves to Death: Public Discourse in the Age of Show Business.* New York: Penguin, 1986.

Purpel, David E., and William M. McLaurin, Jr. *Reflections on the Moral and Spiritual Crisis in Education.* New York: Peter Lang, 2004.

Rest, James R., Muriel J. Bebeau, Mickie Bebeau, Darcia Narvaez, and Stephen J. Thoma. *Postconventional Moral Thinking: A Neo-Kohlbergian Approach.* Mahwah, NJ: Lawrence Erlbaum Associates, 1999.

Rinaldi, Charles. *The Albert Schweitzer Inter-School Service Project.* Wallingford, CT: Albert Schweitzer Institute for the Humanities, 1998.

Rockefeller, Steven C. *John Dewey: Religious Faith and Democratic Humanism.* New York: Columbia University Press, 1991.

Rousseau, Jean-Jacques. *Émile, or On Education.* Translated by Allan Bloom. New York: Basic Books, 1979.

Rud, A. G. "Caring for Others as a Path to Teaching and Learning: Albert Schweitzer's Reverence for Life." In *Ethical Visions of Education: Philosophies in Practice,* edited by David T. Hansen, 157–71. New York: Teachers College Press, 2007.

Rud, Anthony G., Jr. "Learning in Comfort: Developing an Ethos of Hospitality in Education." In *The Educational Conversation: Closing the Gap,* edited by James W. Garrison and Anthony G. Rud Jr., 119–28. Albany: State University of New York Press, 1995.

———. "Breaking the Egg Crate," *Educational Theory* 43(1) (1993): 71–83.

Rud, A. G., and Jim Garrison. "Leading Schools with Reverence," *Educational Forum* 74(2) (2010): 143–57.

Rud, Anthony G., Jr., and Walter P. Oldendorf, eds. *A Place for Teacher Renewal: Challenging the Intellect, Creating Educational Reform,* 1992. Reprint, Charlotte, NC: Information Age Publishing, 2008.

Samuels, Bill. "Overall Goals of the Compassionate Curriculum." Unpublished paper. Harmony, FL: The Harmony Institute, 2006.

Schultz, Katherine. "After the Blackbird Whistles: Listening to Silence in Classrooms," *Teachers College Record,* 113(10) (2011). http://www.tcrecord.org/Issue.asp?volyear=2011&number=10&volume=113

Schweitzer, Albert. *Civilization and Ethics*, in *The Philosophy of Civilization*, translated by C. T. Campion. Amherst, NY: Prometheus Books, 1987.

———. *Essential Writings*. Selected with an introduction by James Brabazon. Maryknoll, NY: Orbis Books, 2005.

———. "Falconry Once More." *In The Animal World of Albert Schweitzer: Jungle Insights into Reverence for Life*, ed. and trans. by Charles R. Joy, 174–179. Boston: Beacon Press, 1951. Originally published as "Nochmals Falkenjägerei," Atlantis (Zurich) (March 1932).

———. *Goethe: Five Studies*. Translated, with an introduction, by Charles R. Joy. Boston: Beacon Press, 1961.

———. *Memoirs of Childhood and Youth*. Translated by C. T. Bergel. New York: Macmillan, 1931. Originally published in English, 1924.

———. *Memoirs of Childhood and Youth*. Translated by Kurt Bergel and Alice R. Bergel. Syracuse, NY: Syracuse University Press, 1997.

———. *Out of My Life and Thought: An Autobiography*. Translated by Antje Bultmann Lemke. Baltimore: Johns Hopkins University Press, 1998.

———. *The Primeval Forest* (Including *On the Edge of the Primeval Forest* and *More from the Primeval Forest*.). 1931. Reprint, Baltimore: Johns Hopkins University Press, 1998.

———. "The Relations of the White and Coloured Races," *The Contemporary Review CXXXIII*, January-June 1928, 65–70.

———. *The Teaching of Reverence for Life*. New York: Holt, Rinehart and Winston, 1965.

Sergiovanni, Thomas J. *The Lifeworld of Leadership: Creating Culture, Community, and Personal Meaning in Our Schools*. San Francisco: Jossey-Bass, 1999.

Silber, Kate. *Pestalozzi: The Man and His Work*. (2nd edition). London: Routledge and Kegan Paul, 1965.

Taylor, Paul C. "Art, Education, and Witness; or, How to Make Our Ideals Clear." In *Philosophy of Education 2009*, ed. Deborah Kerdeman, Barbara Applebaum, Ann Chinnery, Paul Farber, Bob Floden, Diane Gereluk, David Granger, Chris Higgins, Rob Kunzman, Anne Newman, Stephen Norris, Emily Robertson, and Kurt Stemhagen, 25–38. Urbana, IL: Philosophy of Education Society, 2010.

Unitas Fratrum: The Moravian Unity of the World Wide Moravian Church. Origin and Growth of the Unitas Fratrum. http://www.unitasfratrum.org/pages/origin_and_growth.html.

Woodruff, Paul. *Reverence: Renewing a Forgotten Virtue*. New York: Oxford University Press, 2001.

Index

A

accountability 81, 94, 101, 104, 123–25
  culture of 94, 101
  educational 124
  high-stakes 124, 153
Albert Schweitzer
  Center 127, 160
  Colleges 133–34
  Hospital 104
  Institutes 38–39, 127–28, 133–34, 160–61
  Inter-School Service Project 128, 160
Alsace 4–5, 108–9
Anderson, Erica 92, 108, 144, 157
anguish 30, 33–34
awe 10, 15, 55, 57, 61, 69–70, 75–76, 79, 152
  reverential 137

B

Bach, Johann Sebastian 9, 91, 95
Barsam, Ara Paul 21, 23–24, 68, 146, 151–53
Beck, Alan M. 143, 154
Bekoff, Marc 144
beliefs 31, 78, 82–83, 89–90, 132
Bergel, Kurt 144–45, 150, 152, 160
Berliner, David C. 124, 153, 160
Biblical prophets 117–18
Brabazon, James 5, 14, 28, 144–45, 147, 156–57, 159
Bresslau, Hélène 4, 15, 27–38, 67

C

Campbell's law 124
Captain Ahab 77–78

cardinal virtue 56, 62, 78, 81–82, 87
ceremonies
  integrative 83
  naming 76
  shared 73
Chapman University 38–39, 133, 161
character 3–4, 7, 9, 13, 15, 22, 55–56, 69, 72, 80, 82
Christian 9, 19, 22–23, 116
  faith 31, 34, 61
Christianity 9, 13, 19, 22, 35, 113–14, 135
civilization 11, 17, 53–54, 62, 97, 151
classrooms 57, 63, 72, 74–75, 77, 93
Colmar 5, 10, 115
colonialism 96, 102–3, 107, 112–13, 115–16, 140, 145
Comenius, Johann Amos 40, 149
commitment 11, 15, 22, 27, 36–38, 46, 90–91, 105, 114
  ethical 7, 103
community 56, 58, 69, 79, 83, 90, 94, 96, 101, 127, 131
  classroom 58, 73
  of practice 58, 105
  reverent 80
community service 160–61
compassion 23, 56–57, 62–63, 71, 79–81, 85, 94, 162
conscience 7, 94, 118, 122, 139–40
courage 31, 56, 78, 81–82, 129
Cousins, Norman 92, 104, 108, 155–57
cruelty 79, 144

culture 14, 17–18, 56–57, 70, 81,
 83–84, 100, 104, 115
curriculum 113, 117, 124, 127, 129,
 131–32, 134–36
 compassionate 129, 131, 161
customs 116–17
 native 102, 111

D
Deal, Terrence E., and Peterson,
 Kent D. 82–83, 85–86, 154–55
Descartes, René 49, 55, 95, 98
Dewey, John 61, 70, 99–101, 118,
 120, 133, 153, 156–59, 161
Dives and Lazarus 22, 122
dread 123–24
DuBois, W. E. B. 102–3, 157
duty 8–9, 14, 37, 47, 56, 94
dwelling 59, 139, 152

E
education
 community-based 93
 environmental 127
 philosophy of 18, 94, 105, 133
educational
 change 132
 legacy 31, 63, 96, 116–17, 148
 philosophy 5, 18, 105, 133, 161
 theory 3, 113, 116, 135–36
 thought 137, 143
 practices 3, 90, 101, 104, 129, 136
Ehrfurcht vor dem Leben 59
emotions 28, 37, 51, 55–56, 81, 139
 ethical 22
 self-regarding 139
environmental awareness 94, 96, 98–99
eschatology, practical 21, 68
ethical
 action 22, 53, 135, 159
 mysticism 61, 145, 155
ethics 13–15, 24, 50, 54, 58, 62, 79, 137
 boundless 23–24
 of reverence for life 157
 universal guiding 135
 virtue 56, 80

F
faith 5, 9, 31, 35
fear 51, 59, 123
film
 Albert Schweitzer 108
 Le Grand Blanc de Lambaréné 107
Frank, Anne 29, 147

G
Gabon 91, 103, 107, 112, 114, 135, 150
Garrison, Jim 117–18, 151, 153–54,
 156, 159
Glass, Gene V. 124, 160
Goethe, Johann Wolfgang von 13–16,
 23, 61, 67, 100, 104, 145
Goodall, Jane 41, 161
grace 70, 79, 84, 94
gratitude 48–49, 62, 147
Günsbach 5, 108–10
Gunther, John 92–93, 155, 158

H
Hansen, David T. 29, 44–47, 104,
 138–39, 147, 150, 156–57, 162
happiness 35, 37, 56
Harmony Institute 129, 131, 135, 161
Hartle, Ann 95, 156
healing 92–93, 102
heart 8, 13, 19, 30, 33, 35, 52, 122,
 126–27, 138
Heidegger, Martin 59, 122, 152
heroism 91
 no thought of 47
Herrenhüter 5, 40
Hillesum, Ettie 29, 138
hospitality 39, 50, 75, 90–94, 96,
 101–2, 104, 110, 151, 156
hubris 72, 80
human limitation 55, 57, 79–80, 84,
 152
humility 47, 74, 76, 78, 83, 95

I
Ice, Jackson Lee 20, 53, 60, 145–46,
 151–52, 160
idealism, youthful 8, 13–14, 32, 51

imposter virtues 76, 82, 87
Indian thought 16, 23–24, 146, 152
individualism 17–18
individuals, paradigmatic 118–19, 159
irreverence 58, 76, 78

J
Jainism 9, 13, 19, 23, 135, 146, 152
Ahimsâ 24, 134
Jaspers, Karl 108, 118–19, 159–60, 165
Jesus 9, 18–23, 30–31, 33–34, 54, 95,
107, 111, 114, 118, 159
Joy, Charles R. 145, 148, 161
jungle doctor 91, 107–8, 112, 114
justice 56–57, 62, 71, 76, 78–79, 94

K
Kant, Immanuel 8–9, 13–14, 16, 32,
54, 91, 135, 145
kindness 49, 51–52, 102
knowledge 44, 52, 70, 77, 80, 91, 118,
132–33, 135
mutual 49–50
Kraus, Oscar 21–22, 24, 121, 145–46,
160

L
Lambaréné
find their own 95
hospital 47–48, 93
leaders 43, 70, 76, 78–79, 81–87, 131
leadership 68, 77, 79, 87, 90, 131, 154
educational 80, 82, 86
legend 45, 112–13, 136
lifeworld 80–82, 87, 93, 154, 156
listening 59, 71, 74, 78, 86, 102, 149,
153–54
reverential 73

M
making your life your argument 17,
44, 97, 121, 136–37
Marxsen, Patti M. 150, 152, 155, 157
maturity 50–51
medical practices 116–17
megalopsuchia (great-souledness) 95

Memoirs of Childhood and Youth 5,
48, 94, 143–44, 150–51
Messianic consciousness 68
Meyer, Marvin 20, 39, 133, 143,
145–46, 152, 160
Miller, Rhena Schweitzer 27–28, 30,
38–41, 134
mission 19, 25, 35–36, 46, 83, 113,
115, 117–18
missionaries 35, 43, 97, 122
Moby-Dick 77, 154
Montague, J. F. 92, 112, 156–58, 162
Montaigne, Michel de 95, 156
moral
education 89, 91, 93–95, 97, 99,
101, 103, 105
imagination 56, 89–90, 114, 155
morality 14, 63, 90, 96
Moravian Brethren 5, 40
More, Sir Thomas 113, 140, 162
Munz, Walter 150, 157
music 5, 9–10, 33
musician 4, 31, 35, 95, 138–39
mystery 49–50, 57, 59, 75, 83, 85–87

N
natural piety 61, 99, 101, 153
NCCAT (North Carolina Center
for the Advancement of
Teaching) 77, 143
Nietzsche, Friedrich 13, 16–19, 31,
44, 95, 122
Nobel Peace Prize 103, 110, 135–36,
139

O
Ogooué River 54, 109, 135

P
parenthood 126
parenting 125–26
Paris Missionary Society 18, 34–35,
43, 91
passion 18–19, 85, 117
Payne, Robert 104, 116–17, 152, 157,
159

peace 135
performativity 123–25
pessimism 16–17, 53, 160
Pestalozzi, Johann Heinrich 126–27,
    160
philosophers 13–15, 17, 94, 97, 99,
    135
philosophy 5, 13, 16, 24, 40, 53–54,
    95, 100, 110, 113, 137
Philosophy of Education Society 157
piety 40, 61
    appropriate 79
    simple 5
positionality 125
practical reverence 62–63, 68, 82–83,
    87, 89, 135, 137, 156
principles
    bedrock 53, 97
    guiding 23, 130
prophecy 17–18, 117
    educational 159
prophet 18, 118
    educational 18, 108, 117
Purpel, David 108, 117–18, 159

Q
Quinnipiac University 38, 41, 134, 161

R
reason 9, 14, 17–18, 51, 53
recovery project 107–8
redemption 47, 68
Reflections on the Moral and Spiritual
    Crisis in Education 159
religion 5, 9, 13, 23–25, 32, 55, 57, 61,
    77, 83, 113–15, 159
respect 23, 50, 55, 57–60, 69, 71, 73–
    74, 79, 85, 87, 98, 105, 129–30
responsibility 16, 59, 77, 98, 101, 134
responsibilization 125
reverence 55–59, 61–62, 68–69, 71,
    73–83, 85–87, 100, 137
    definition of 55
    natural 78
    object of 57–58, 79
    religious 77

Reverence for Life 53–55, 57–63, 67,
    80, 85, 90, 100, 126, 134, 144–46,
    152
    ethic of 99, 133
    philosophy of 100, 104, 128
    practice of 89, 135
    principle of 98–99
reverent 57, 69, 76, 78–80, 82, 86
    attitude 79, 86
    classrooms 58
    deliberation 87
    educational leadership 82, 86
    humility 80, 87
    inquiry 86
    leaders 77–78, 83–84, 86
    leadership 77, 80
    listening 70–72, 74
    moments 75
    rituals 83, 85
    school culture 80
    teachers 58, 69–73
    traits 69
ritual and ceremony 55–56, 58, 69,
    73, 75, 77, 80–85, 87
rituals
    closing 85
    common 84
    daily 73
    empty 85
    extended hospitality 75
Rousseau, Jean-Jacques 63, 127
Rud, Anthony G. 143, 150–51,
    153–54, 156

S
school
    common 68
    community 76, 87
    culture 73, 81–82, 87
    leaders 77, 79–82, 87, 89, 94, 96,
        101, 104
    pluralistic 86
the school will be the way 136–37,
    148
schoolhome 104, 157, 166
schoolmaster's blood 136

Schopenhauer, Arthur 13, 16–17, 23
Schultz, Katherine 72, 74, 154
Schweitzer
  hagiographic 108
  influence upon education 133, 136
  legacy 120, 126
  legend 6, 107, 158
  myth 105, 107–8, 112, 136
  schools 113
  spirit 105
Schweitzer, Adèle 4
Schweitzer, Louis 4
Schweitzer's
  character 22, 28–29, 90
  childhood 4, 6
  daughter. See Miller, Rhena
    Schweitzer
  decision to go to Africa 43–44
  hospital 103, 116
  influence 117, 127, 133, 136, 159
  isolation 116
  legacy 119
  life 104, 127, 134
  life project 110
  magnanimity 95
  medical practice 102
  motivation 27
  Nobel Peace Prize 135
  philosophy 94, 100, 131–32
  solitariness 113
  thoughts 111, 129
  value 117, 137
  wife. See Bresslau, Hélène
  work 90, 94, 101, 115, 117, 136

Sergiovanni, Thomas J. 80, 82, 84, 87,
  154, 156
shame 6, 8, 55, 58
silence 72, 74, 154
Socrates 113–14, 118–19, 159
spirit 78, 83, 85, 127
spiritual decay 17
strangers 50, 116, 123
systemsworld 80–81, 83, 87

T
teacher
  educators 96, 104, 150
  renewal 143, 150, 154
teachers
  expert 91
  good 70
  honored 75
teaching
  reverence 162
thinking 31, 45, 54, 59, 89–90,
  97–98
traditions 83, 125

V
vocation 18, 44–45, 47, 96, 104

W
Wir epigones (we inheritors of the
  past) 10, 115
wisdom 70, 85
  practical 56
Woodruff, Paul 56–57, 71, 74, 78,
  152–55